This book is dedicated to all who are
FRIENDS OF ROTARY
and to those who will become friends of
Rotary because of what they see among these
images—Fellowship, Service, and Peace.

Dedicamos este libro a todos los
AMIGOS DE ROTARY
y a todos aquellos que se harán
amigos de Rotary al contemplar
estas imágenes ilustrativas del
Compañerismo, el Servicio y la Paz.

Ce livre est dédié à tous les
AMIS DU ROTARY
et à tous ceux qui en deviendront les amis
pour avoir vu ces
images de camaraderie, de service et de paix.

Rotary International
Headquarters
One Rotary Center, Evanston,
Illinois, U.S.A.

Sede de Rotary International,
One Rotary Center, Evanston,
Illinois, EEUU.

Siège du Rotary International
One Rotary Center, Evanston,
Illinois, U.S.A.

IMAGES OF ROTARY
A World Imagined

IMAGENES DE ROTARY
La esperanza de un mundo mejor

IMAGES DU ROTARY
Imaginez un monde . . .

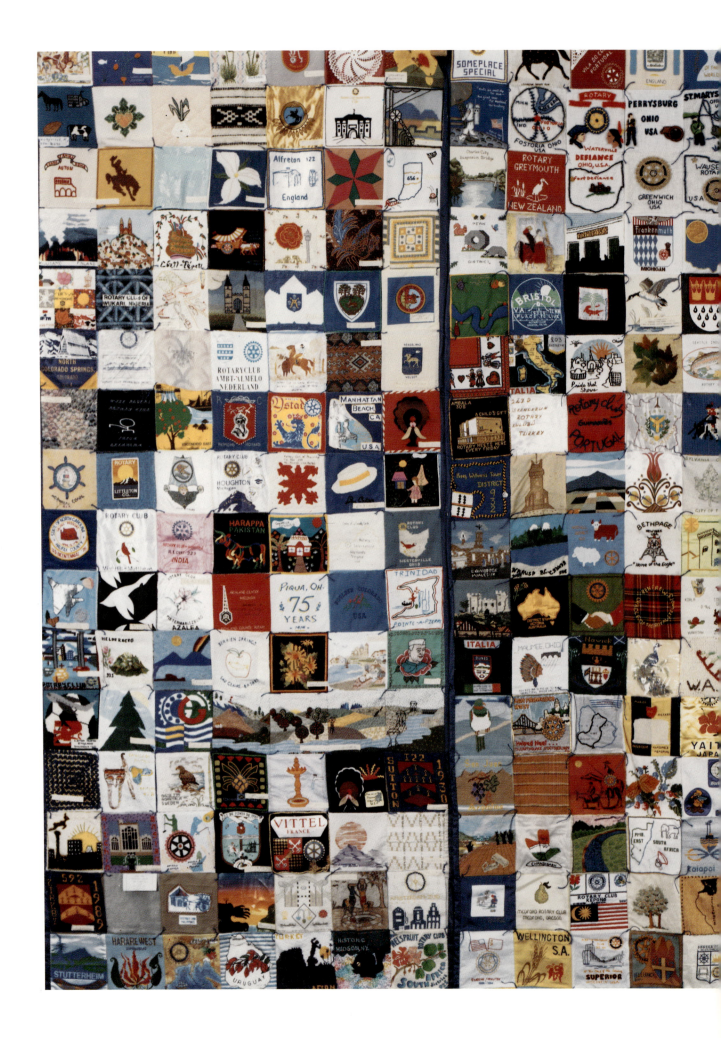

The Great Rotary Tapestry, created for the 1990 International Convention, is a collage of 1,600 colorful blocks reflecting the unity of Rotary International in the diversity of its 25,000-plus clubs worldwide.

El gran tapiz de Rotary, creado para la convención internacional de 1990, es un collage compuesto por 1.600 coloridos retazos de género, a través del cual se refleja la unidad de Rotary International coexistente con la diversidad de sus más de 25.000 clubes del mundo entero.

La grande tapisserie du Rotary, créée en vue du Congrès 1990, est une mosaïque de 1 600 carrés de tissus chatoyants représentant l'unité du Rotary International dans la diversité de ses plus de 25 000 clubs de par le monde.

Editor/Redacción/Rédaction: Janet Boyd
Designer/Diseño/Direction artistique: Pelayia Limbos
Artists/Artes gráficas/Arts graphiques: Cynthia Cleland, timeline/cronología/chronologie; Linda Perry, map/mapa/carte; Mimi Gross, keyline pasteup/maquetación/maquette
Photo Researchers/Selección fotográfica/Recherche de photographies: Jacqueline Oliven, Beth Pearson
Translators/Traductores/Traductions:
French/francés/Français —Corine Fortunato, Jacques Lacava; Proof readers/correctores/Correcteurs: Michèle Moiron, Jean-Mathieu Diebold
Japanese/japonés/Japonais —Shunjo Takahashi, Yoshi Watanabe
Portuguese/portugués/Portugais —Ethel Goldenstein
Spanish/español/Espagnol —Eytán Lasca
Production Coordinators/Coordinadoras de producción/Coordinatrices: Charlene Sobczak, Hollie Horn
Project Supervisor/Supervisor de proyecto/Chef de projet: F. Paige Carlin
Communications Division Manager/Gerente de la División de Comunicaciones/Responsable de la division des Communications: Willmon L. White

Library of Congress Catalog Card No. 91-061665/ISBN 0-915062-25-9

IMAGES OF ROTARY is published in two editions:
Rotary International Publication No. CD3-293-MU is in English, French and Spanish
Rotary International Publication No. CD3-294-MU is in English, Japanese and Portuguese
Books may be ordered directly from the publisher:
Rotary International, One Rotary Center, 1560 Sherman Avenue, Evanston, Illinois, U.S.A. 60201.

Biblioteca del Congreso de los EEUU, No. de catálogo 91-061665/ISBN 0-915062-25-9

IMAGENES DE ROTARY se publica en dos ediciones:
La publicación de Rotary International No. CD3-293-MU, en español, francés e inglés.
La publicación de Rotary International No. CD3-294-MU, en inglés, japonés y portugués.
Solicite ejemplares directamente al editor: Rotary International, One Rotary Center, 1560 Sherman, Evanston, Illinois 60201, EEUU.

Library of Congress Catalog Card No. 91-061665/ISBN 0-915062-25-9

IMAGES DU ROTARY est publié en deux versions:
Publication du Rotary International No. CD3-293-MU en anglais, français et espagnol.
Publication du Rotary International No. CD3-294-MU en anglais, japonais et portugais.
Les livres peuvent être directement commandés auprès de l'éditeur:
Rotary International, One Rotary Center, 1560 Sherman Avenue, Evanston, Illinois, Etats-Unis 60 201.

Contents

Indice

Table des matières

Introduction

I believe that *Images of Rotary* is a book whose time has come. It builds on a tradition begun in 1975, when *The World of Rotary* was published in honor of our 70th anniversary. In the years since then, the Rotary world has grown and changed in ways we could never have foreseen. In 1975, we only dreamed of the day when Eastern Europe would return to the Rotary world. Our doors were not yet open to women. PolioPlus was still in the future. Today, our horizons of service have expanded. Preserve Planet Earth has moved from dream to reality. These stories—and the news of our growing service to education, literacy, health issues, and young people—need to be told.

We are on the brink of the 21st century. As international president, I felt we were again ready to *Honor Rotary* by showing our true image to the world. The R.I. Board of Directors supported this idea, and *Images of Rotary* was born. We agreed that we live in an age of visual communications, so we decided to create an up-to-the-minute history of Rotary—its unity and internationality, its dedication to peace and goodwill and service—through a gallery of meaningful images.

You hold the result in your hands . . . a treasury of colorful and dramatic story-telling photos from all parts of the Rotary world. In these images you will see the many aspects of Rotary life, and the many ways that lives are touched and enhanced by this remarkable organization. For the most part, the pictures speak for themselves, but you will also find historical information and concise descriptions of Rotary programs.

This book will be a favorite both with Rotarians and friends of Rotary. I hope that Rotarians will share these images with others, present a copy to visiting dignitaries and special guests, donate this volume to local libraries and schools, and display it proudly. As a portfolio of Rotary service, it will make new friends for Rotary and will help to make our true image more widely known and understood.

Many people have helped to make *Images of Rotary* a reality, and I would like to express my thanks. First, my appreciation goes to the countless uncredited photographers—amateurs and professionals—whose work you see in this book. Many thanks also to the Secretariat staff and the editors of our regional Rotary publications for their ideas, photographs, and inspiration. Finally, my gratitude to two special people: Rotarian Willmon L. White, who understood my vision for this project and brought it to fruition; and R.I. Director Richard D. King, chairman of the 1990-91 executive committee, for his enthusiastic introduction of the book at the 1991 International Convention in Mexico City.

Paulo V.C. Costa
President, Rotary International

Introducción

Creo que ha llegado la hora de que saliera un libro como *Imágenes de Rotary*. Se basa en una tradición que data de 1975, año de publicación de *El mundo de Rotary*, en honor a nuestro 70º aniversario. Durante los dieciséis años transcurridos desde aquel entonces, el mundo de Rotary ha crecido y cambiado en una medida que ni siquiera habríamos podido predecir. En 1975 la posibilidad de que un día Europa Oriental regresara al mundo rotario no era más que un hermoso sueño. En aquel entonces, nuestras puertas no estaban aún abiertas a las mujeres, y PolioPlus pertenecía enteramente al futuro. En la actualidad, se han ampliado enormemente nuestros horizontes de servicio. El programa Preservemos el Planeta Tierra, ha dejado de ser un sueño para convertirse en una realidad. Estas historias, y las noticias sobre nuestro creciente servicio en pro de la educación, la alfabetización, la salud, y la juventud, tienen que ser debidamente difundidas.

Estamos en los albores del siglo XXI. Como presidente internacional, creo que estamos nuevamente preparados para *Valorizar Rotary* revelando nuestra verdadera imagen ante el mundo. La Junta Directiva de RI apoyó esta idea, y así nació *Imágenes de Rotary*. Partiendo de la base de que vivimos en una era de comunicaciones visuales, decidimos crear una reseña sobre Rotary actualizada al máximo, dando fe de su unidad e internacionalidad, su dedicación a la causa de la paz, la buena voluntad y el servicio, a través de una espléndida galería de significativas imágenes.

Este libro será uno de los favoritos, tanto para los rotarios como para los amigos de Rotary. Espero que los rotarios compartan estas imágenes con los demás, obsequien un ejemplar a los dignatarios e invitados especiales que visiten su club, donen este volumen a las escuelas y bibliotecas de la localidad, y lo difundan con orgullo. Como muestra del servicio rotario, contribuirá a que Rotary gane nuevos amigos y a que nuestra verdadera imagen se conozca y comprenda mucho más ampliamente.

Son muchos los que han ayudado a que *Imágenes de Rotary* sea hoy una realidad; quisiera al respecto agradecerles como corresponde. En primer lugar mi más sincero aprecio por los innumerables fotógrafos anónimos (profesionales y aficionados) cuyos trabajos se incluyen en este libro. Quisiera también expresar mi agradecimiento al personal de la Secretaría y los directores de nuestras publicaciones regionales de Rotary, por sus ideas, fotografías e inspiración. Final-

mente, mi más profunda gratitud a dos personas en especial: el Rotario Willmon L. White, quien comprendió cabalmente mi visión de este proyecto y supo llevarla a la realidad; y al Director de RI Richard D. King, presidente del Comité Ejecutivo de 1990-91, por su entusiasta presentación de la obra ante la convención internacional de 1991 en la Ciudad de México.

Paulo V. C. Costa
Presidente, Rotary International

Introduction

Je crois que la publication de ce livre vient à point nommé. Il repose sur une tradition qui a débuté en 1975, lorsque *The World of Rotary* a été publié en l'honneur de notre 70ème anniversaire. Dans les années qui suivirent, le monde du Rotary s'est étendu et modifié de manière imprévisible. En 1975, nous ne pouvions que rêver du jour où l'Europe de l'Est reviendrait dans le monde du Rotary. Nos portes n'étaient pas encore ouvertes aux femmes. PolioPlus appartenait au futur. Aujourd'hui, nos horizons de service se sont élargis. Le programme Protégeons notre planète est passé du rêve à la réalité. Ces histoires, et les chroniques de nos activités au service de la jeunesse, de l'éducation, de l'alphabétisation, ainsi que celles touchant aux problèmes de santé, demandent à être racontées.

Nous sommes à la veille du 21ème siècle. En tant que Président, j'ai pensé que nous étions à nouveau prêts à valoriser le Rotary en présentant notre véritable image au monde. Le Conseil Central du RI a soutenu cette idée, et "Images du Rotary" est né. Nous avons unanimement constaté que nous vivons dans un âge de communication visuelle, donc nous avons décidé de créer un historique récent du Rotary, de son unité et de son internationalité, de son attachement à la paix, à la bonne volonté et au service, sous la forme d'une compilation de photos significatives.

Vous tenez le résultat entre vos mains . . . une myriade de photos évocatrices, colorées et pleines d'action, de tous les coins du monde rotarien. Dans ces images vous observerez les nombreux aspects de la vie du Rotary, et les nombreuses façons par lesquelles des vies sont changées grâce à cette remarquable organisation. Dans la plupart des cas, les photos parlent d'elles-mêmes, et vous trouverez également des éléments historiques et des descriptions concises des programmes du Rotary.

Ce livre connaîtra un grand succès auprès des Rotariens et des amis du Rotary. J'espère que vous partagerez ces images avec d'autres, présenterez cet ouvrage aux personnalités rotariennes en visite et aux invités d'honneur, offrirez ce livre aux écoles et aux bibliothèques, et le mettrez avec fierté en évidence aux yeux de tous. Témoignage du service rotarien, il nous permettra d'acquérir de nouveaux amis au Rotary et rendra notre véritable image plus connue et mieux comprise.

De nombreuses personnes ont contribué à la réalisation d'*Images du Rotary*, et j'aimerais leur exprimer ma gratitude. Tout d'abord, mes remerciements vont aux nombreux photographes, amateurs et professionnels, dont vous voyez le travail dans ce livre. Merci infiniment au personnel du Secrétariat et aux directeurs de nos magazines régionaux pour leurs idées, photographies, et inspiration. Enfin, toute ma gratitude va à deux personnes remarquables: le Rotarien Willmon L. White, qui a compris ma vision pour ce projet et lui a permis de voir le jour ; et le Directeur du RI Richard D. King, président de la commission exécutive 1990-91, pour sa présentation enthousiaste du livre au Congrès International de Mexico.

Paulo V.C. Costa
Président du Rotary International

PREFACE

Imagine a world of service . . . imagine a world without need. Imagine a world of children unfettered by crippling disease. Imagine a world of plenty, where hunger is long forgotten. Imagine a world of natural beauty, where mighty trees frame the sky. Look at the world around you—and then imagine what it could be . . .

See images of pain comforted, illness conquered, poverty held firmly at bay. Picture trees and crops as they rise on once-parched soil, and water running clear in the desert. Visualize barriers coming down, and hands joined in friendship across international boundaries. See reflections of peace, of honor, and world understanding, as culture meets culture in the common bond of service. Observe the modern world of Rotary through eyes that have seen it in action.

The scenes in *Images of Rotary: A World Imagined* grow out of an attitude of hope and faith—a determination to work for goals not easily attainable, and the human capacity to dream . . . More importantly, they represent the struggle to make dreams a reality. Take a moment, and spend some time with the Rotarians on these pages. Look into their lives of service— and share their enthusiasm for serving mankind.

Come envision a day of dignity for all the world's people. See our planet move into the 21st century, green and

PREFACIO

Imagine un mundo de servicio . . . imagine un mundo sin carencias. Imagine un mundo en el cual los niños no teman quedar paralizados por una terrible enfermedad. Imagine un mundo de abundancia, en el cual haya sido olvidado el fantasma del hambre. Imagine un mundo en el cual reine la belleza natural, y se divisen imponentes los árboles sobre el horizonte de un cielo azul. Observe el mundo que nos rodea y, a continuación, imagine cómo podría ser . . .

Vea estas imágenes de alivio ante el dolor, derrota de las enfermedades, y de lucha contra la pobreza. Imagine árboles y cultivos desarrollándose donde anteriormente no había más que áridos terrenos calcinados por el sol; y vea también fluir el agua por el desierto. Visualice el derribamiento de las barreras al unirse seres humanos mediante lazos de amistad que superan todas las fronteras internacionales. Vea los reflejos de la paz, la dignidad, y la comprensión internacional, a medida que se ponen en contacto diversas culturas mediante el vínculo común del servicio. Observe el mundo moderno de Rotary a través de los ojos que lo han visto en acción.

Las escenas de *IMAGE-NES DE ROTARY la esperanza de un mundo mejor,* derivan de una actitud de fe y esperanza, de una decisión de trabajar en pro de metas no fácilmente alcanzables, y de la capacidad que el ser humano tiene para soñar . . . Es mucho más importante aún mencionar que representan la lucha por llevar los sueños a la realidad. Aproveche esta oportunidad para pasar momentos sumamente interesantes junto a los

PREFACE

Imaginez un monde de service . . . imaginez un monde sans besoins. Imaginez un monde où les enfants ne souffriraient pas de maladies paralysantes. Imaginez un monde d'abondance, où la faim serait depuis longtemps oubliée. Imaginez un monde de beauté naturelle, où des arbres vigoureux se profileraient sur l'azur. Regardez le monde autour de vous - et puis imaginez ce qu'il pourrait être . . .

Percevez des images de souffrances soulagées, de maladies vaincues, de pauvreté tenue à distance. Voyez des arbres et des récoltes poussant sur des sols jadis stériles, et de l'eau claire ruisselant dans le désert. Imaginez les barrières abolies et les poignées de mains, geste d'amitié par dessus les frontières. Voyez les reflets de la paix, de l'honneur, de l'entente mondiale, tandis que les civilisations communient dans le lien commun du service. Observez le monde moderne du Rotary avec des yeux qui l'ont déjà vu en action.

Ces scènes dans *Images du Rotary : Imaginez un monde . . .* proviennent d'une attitude d'espérance et de foi — la détermination de travailler à des buts difficilement réalisables, et la faculté de rêver . . . Plus important, elles représentent le combat qui métamorphose le rêve en réalité. Prenez un moment, et passez quelque temps avec les Rotariens de ces pages. Entrez dans leurs vies consacrées au service et partagez leur enthousiasme pour servir l'humanité.

Envisager le jour où tous les peuples du monde auront droit à la dignité. Voyez notre planète faire son entrée dans le

peaceful with hope for the future. See the Rotary world as it is—and as it is becoming. Imagine a world of service above self. Imagine more than you thought could be imagined, and more than you ever dared dream. Let your imagination soar . . . Imagine a world of Rotary . . .

rotarios, a través de estas páginas. Sepa apreciar su vida dedicada al servicio, y comparta su entusiasmo por servir a la humanidad.

Acuda a forjar una visión de una jornada de dignidad para toda la población mundial. Vea a nuestro planeta avanzar hacia el siglo XXI, en paz y pletórico de zonas verdes, con esperanza de cara al futuro. Vea el mundo de Rotary tal cual es . . . y tal cual se está transformando. Imagine un mundo basado en la máxima de dar de sí antes de pensar en sí. Imagine mucho más de lo que usted creía posible imaginar. Deje elevar su imaginación hacia alturas insospechadas . . . Imagine un mundo de Rotary . . .

21ème siècle, verte et paisible avec un avenir plein d'espoir. Voyez le monde du Rotary tel qu'il est, et tel qu'il devient. Imaginez un monde où règne la devise "Servir d'abord". Imaginez plus encore que possible, et rêvez plus que vous n'auriez jamais osé. Laissez votre imagination s'envoler . . . vers un monde rotarien.

Object of Rotary

The Object of Rotary is to encourage and foster the ideal of service as a basis of worthy enterprise and, in particular, to encourage and foster:

First. The development of acquaintance as an opportunity for service;

Second. High ethical standards in business and professions; the recognition of the worthiness of all useful occupations; and the dignifying by each Rotarian of his occupation as an opportunity to serve society;

Third. The application of the ideal of service by every Rotarian to his personal, business, and community life;

Fourth. The advancement of international understanding, goodwill, and peace through a world fellowship of business and professional persons united in the ideal of service.

Objetivo de Rotary

El Objetivo de Rotary es estimular y fomentar el ideal de servicio como base de toda empresa digna y, en particular, estimular y fomentar:

Primero: El conocimiento mutuo y la amistad como ocasión de servir.

Segundo: La buena fe como norma en los negocios y en las profesiones; el aprecio de toda ocupación útil y la dignificación de la propia en servicio de la sociedad.

Tercero: La aplicación del ideal de servicio por todos los rotarios a su vida privada, profesional y pública.

Cuarto: La inteligencia, la buena voluntad y la paz entre las naciones por el compañerismo de sus personas de negocios y profesionales, unidas en el ideal de servicio.

But du Rotary

Le But du Rotary consiste à encourager et à cultiver l'idéal de servir considéré comme base de toute entreprise honorable, et en particulier à encourager et à cultiver:

Premièrement. Le développement des relations personnelles d'amitié entre ses membres en vue de leur fournir des occasions de servir l'intérêt général;

Deuxièmement. L'observation de règles de haute probité et de délicatesse dans l'exercice de toute profession; la reconnaissance de la dignité de toute occupation utile; l'effort pour honorer sa profession et en élever le niveau de manière à mieux servir la société;

Troisièmement. L'application de l'idéal de servir par tout Rotarien dans sa vie personnelle, professionnelle et sociale;

Quatrièmement. La compréhension mutuelle internationale, la bonne volonté et l'amour de la paix en créant et en entretenant à travers le monde des relations cordiales entre les représentants des diverses professions, unis dans l'idéal de servir.

Rotary Mottoes

"Service Above Self"
"He Profits Most Who Serves Best"

Lemas rotarios

"Dar de sí antes de pensar en sí"
"Se beneficia más el que mejor sirve"

Devises du Rotary

Servir d'abord
Qui sert le mieux profite le plus

IMAGINE THE WORLD AT PEACE
IMAGINEMOS UN MUNDO EN PAZ
IMAGINEZ UN MONDE EN PAIX

The ideal of peace often seems remote, an elusive hope amid the world's divergent political systems, economic policies, cultural values, and religious traditions.

In 1988, Rotary began a series of Peace Forums, enabling people from around the world to discuss problems and seek common goals.

En 1988, Rotary dio comienzo a una serie de Foros para la Paz, dando oportunidad a gente de todas partes del mundo, a discutir problemas y trabajar en pos de objetivos en común.

En 1988, le Rotary a amorcé une série de Forums pour la paix permettant à des personnes du monde entier de discuter de problèmes et de chercher des objectifs communs.

El ideal de paz, a menudo nos parece algo muy remoto, dadas las divergencias existentes en el mundo entre los diversos regímenes políticos y sistemas económicos, valores culturales y tradiciones religiosas.

L'idéal de paix semble tenir peu de place parmi les systèmes politiques divergents du monde, les politiques économiques, les valeurs culturelles et les traditions religieuses.

How do we negotiate our differences? How do we discover points of agreement? How do we live peaceably together?

¿Cómo es posible negociar para solucionar los desacuerdos? ¿Cómo puede hallarse puntos en común para vivir en armonía? ¿Cómo podríamos vivir todos juntos en paz?

Comment aborder nos différends ? Comment découvrir des terrains d'entente ? Comment vivre ensemble en paix ?

4

Rotarians believe that world harmony begins, quite simply, with friendship.

Los rotarios creen que la concordia mundial comienza por algo tan sencillo como la amistad.

Les Rotariens croient que
l'harmonie dans le monde
débute tout simplement par
l'amitié.

It evolves as we get to know people who are different from ourselves and try to imagine what it might be like to live as they do. Peace requires a willingness to accept differences and discern commonalities. It begins with venturing outside one's own world and becoming a little vulnerable.

La paz mundial se va haciendo realidad a medida que conocemos gente diferente a nosotros e intentamos imaginar cómo sería adoptar su forma de vida. Para vivir en paz hace falta estar dispuesto a aceptar las diferencias y reconocer las semejanzas. La paz comienza al aventurarnos fuera de nuestro propio mundo con la consecuente vulnerabilidad que ello implica.

Elle grandit à mesure que nous rencontrons des gens différents de nous et que nous envisageons ce que vivre comme eux signifie. La paix nécessite une volonté d'accepter les différences et de discerner les points communs. Elle commence lorsque l'on s'aventure en dehors de son propre monde et que l'on devient un peu vulnérable.

8

It grows with the discovery that music and laughter are universal languages and that play fosters friendship.

Surge al descubrir que la música y la risa son idiomas universales y que los juegos fomentan la amistad.

L'entente s'accroît avec la découverte que la musique et le rire sont des langages universels et que le jeu stimule l'amitié.

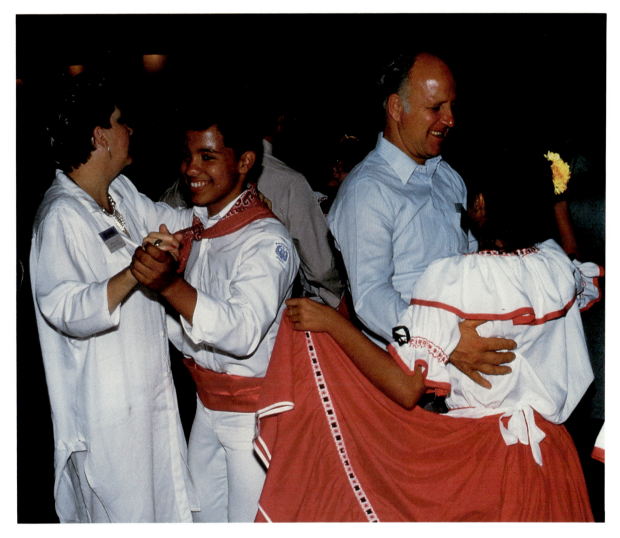

People from all over the world mingle and get to know one another at Rotary's international conventions, regional meetings, and youth conferences. Peace Forums, Conferences for Development, and President's Conferences of Goodwill bring representatives from various countries together to address existing tensions and exchange viewpoints on topics of concern.

Las convenciones internacionales de Rotary International, las reuniones regionales y conferencias para la juventud dan ocasión a que la gente se conozca. Los Foros para la Paz, las conferencias para el desarrollo, y las conferencias presidenciales de buena voluntad reúnen a representantes de diversos países para intentar solucionar las tensiones existentes e intercambiar puntos de vista sobre determinados temas de interés.

Des gens venant des quatre coins du monde font connaissance aux congrès du Rotary International, aux réunions régionales, et aux conférences pour les jeunes. Les forums de la paix, les conférences sur le développement, et les conférences de la bonne volonté du président rassemblent des représentants de divers pays pour aborder les tensions existantes et échanger des points de vue sur des sujets d'inquiétude spécifiques.

Philippine President Corazon Aquino addressed Rotary's 1987 Conference for Development.

En 1987, Corazón Aquino, presidenta de las Filipinas, dirigió la palabra en ocasión de la Conferencia de Rotary para el Desarrollo.

La Présidente des Philippines Corazon Aquino lors d'un discours à la Conférence du développement du Rotary en 1987.

Honored for upholding the principle of respect for all persons, Pope John Paul II received the 1982 Rotary Award for World Understanding from 1981-82 R.I. President Stanley E. McCaffrey.

Debido a su consecuente apoyo al principio del respeto a todas las personas, en 1982, el Papa Juan Pablo II recibió el Premio de Rotary pro Comprensión Mundial, de manos de Stanley McCaffrey, presidente de RI.

Honoré pour avoir soutenu le principe du respect envers toutes les personnes, le Pape Jean Paul II reçoit le Prix de l'entente mondiale du Rotary en 1982 des mains du Président du RI Stanley McCaffrey.

Instigated by Rotarians of Canada and the U.S.A., Glacier-Waterton International Peace Park sits astride the unfortified border of the two countries, indicated only by a 20-foot path through the woods and a stone marker.

Fundado por rotarios de los EEUU y Canadá, el Parque Internacional de la Paz del Glaciar Waterton, está situado sobre la propia frontera entre ambos países, marcada solamente por un indicador de piedra y un sendero de veinte pies a través de los árboles.

A l'instigation des Rotariens du Canada et des Etats-Unis, le parc international de la paix du glacier Waterton est situé sur la frontière ouverte des deux pays, indiquée uniquement par un chemin de 6 mètres à travers les bois et par une pierre commémorative.

Paulo Costa, 1990-91 Rotary International president, receives the Condor of the Andes award for his efforts to promote peace.

Paulo Costa, presidente de Rotary International en 1990-91, recibe el premio Cóndor de los Andes por sus gestiones en pro de la paz.

Paulo Costa, Président du Rotary International en 1990-91, reçoit la récompense du Condor des Andes pour ses efforts de promotion de la paix.

Widely recognized as an organization that promotes global understanding, Rotary International and many individual Rotarians have been honored with prestigious peace awards. Likewise, Rotary presents its own Award for World Understanding and Peace to individuals and organizations who exemplify its vision of peace through selfless service to others. The establishment of peace parks and bridges of peace across borders of neighboring countries gives further testimony to Rotary's goal of cooperation and camaraderie between nations.

Ampliamente reconocida por su calidad de organización dedicada a promover la comprensión a nivel global, Rotary International y numerosos rotarios se han hecho acreedores a prestigiosos galardones debido a su labor en pro de la paz. De la misma manera, Rotary otorga su propio Premio pro Comprensión Mundial a individuos y organizaciones que hayan demostrado su visión pacificadora, brindando a los demás su desinteresado servicio. El establecimiento de parques y puentes para la paz a través de las fronteras entre países vecinos, constituye otro claro ejemplo de que uno de los fines primordiales de Rotary consiste en lograr la cooperación y la camaradería entre las naciones.

Unanimement reconnue comme une organisation qui promeut l'entente mondiale, le Rotary International et de nombreux Rotariens ont été honorés par de prestigieuses récompenses pour la paix. De même, le Rotary décerne son propre prix pour l'entente et la paix mondiales à des personnes ou des organisations qui donnent l'exemple de sa vision pacifiste par un service altruiste. La création de parcs et de ponts de la paix aux frontières de pays voisins représente un témoignage supplémentaire du but du Rotary : la coopération et la camaraderie entre nations.

At the core of Rotary's international focus is The Rotary Foundation. In addition to its extensive youth scholarship program and humanitarian service projects, the Foundation sponsors the Group Study Exchange program, sending teams of young professionals to immerse themselves in the business practices and cultures of other countries. Rotary's people-to-people approach to peace has long been instru-

mental in forging new understandings between nations. In 1987, Rotarian families were hosts to 160 young civic leaders who were among the first groups of Soviet citizens to visit the United States.

Uno de los principales centros de atención por parte de Rotary es La Fundación Rotaria. Además de sus amplios programas de becas, y de proyectos de servicio humanitario, la Fundación patrocina el programa de Intercambio de Grupos de Estudio, mediante el cual se envía a equipos compuestos por jóvenes profesionales y personas de negocios a que efectúen giras de estudio en otras naciones, a fin de que adquieran valiosa información sobre la actividad profesional o empresarial en los respectivos países anfitriones, y también sobre la cultura de los mismos. El contacto persona a persona que Rotary practica, ha sido durante mucho tiempo fundamental para trazar nuevas rutas para la comprensión entre las naciones. En 1988, fueron justamente familias rotarias las que hospedaron a 160 jóvenes líderes cívicos de la URSS, uno de los primeros grupos de ciudadanos soviéticos que visitaron los Estados Unidos.

La Fondation Rotary évoque l'aspect international du Rotary. En plus de son vaste programme de bourses d'études pour jeunes et de projets de service humanitaires, la Fondation parraine le programme d'Echanges de groupes d'étude, composés d'équipes de jeunes adultes qui s'initient aux pratiques professionnelles et cultures étrangères. Le rapprochement des peuples grâce au Rotary a depuis longtemps permis de forger une nouvelle compréhension entre les nations et d'oeuvrer en vue de la paix. En 1987, des familles rotariennes accueillirent 160 jeunes professionnels d'Union Soviétique, qui constituaient les premiers groupes de citoyens soviétiques à visiter les Etats-Unis.

R.I. President Hugh Archer's visits to the Soviet Union in 1989-90 climaxed in the chartering of the Rotary Club of Moscow, first ever in that country.

El Presidente de RI Hugh Archer efectúa en 1989-90 una visita a la Unión Soviética, acontecimiento que se vio culminado por el otorgamiento de la carta constitutiva al Club Rotario de Moscú, el primero en fundarse en dicha nación.

Les visites du Président du RI Hugh Archer en Union Soviétique en 1989-90 ont abouti à la remise de la charte au Rotary club de Moscou, le premier du pays.

17

Wherever there are Rotarians, fellowship and food go together. At banquets, small dinner parties, or around a kitchen table, Rotarians have discovered that sampling the cuisine of another country nurtures the soul as well as the body.

Dondequiera que haya rotarios, podrá disfrutarse a la vez el compañerismo y la comida. A través de numerosos almuerzos, cenas, fiestas, o simplemente ante una mesa de una cocina, los rotarios han descubierto que la degustación de las especialidades gastronómicas de los demás países nutre a la par al cuerpo y al alma.

Partout où il y a des Rotariens, on trouve camaraderie et repas. A des banquets, à des petits dîners, ou autour d'une table de cuisine, les Rotariens ont découvert que de goûter à la cuisine d'un autre pays nourrit l'esprit ainsi que le corps.

19

Through this variety of shared experiences, individual men and women are exposed to the circumstances and perspectives of others and find their own lives enlarged and enriched. By creating opportunities for people to work together, play together, or just be together . . .

Compartiendo experiencias tan diversas, se le brinda a cada persona la posibilidad de experimentar las mismas circunstancias que los demás y considerar sus puntos de vista. Estos contactos amplían y enriquecen su propia vida. Al crear oportunidades para que diversos individuos trabajen juntos, jueguen juntos, o sencillamente estén juntos. . .

En partageant une variété d'expériences, des hommes et des femmes sont exposés à des perspectives différentes et leur propre vie s'en trouve enrichie et élargie. En permettant que les gens travaillent ensemble, jouent ensemble, ou tout simplement soient ensemble. . .

. . . Rotary helps the world envision itself at peace.

. . . Rotary ayuda a que el mundo entero tenga una idea de lo que podría ser un mundo en paz.

. . . le Rotary aide le monde à s'imaginer en paix.

22

IMAGINE! A WORLD LESS HUNGRY, LESS POOR, LESS LONELY, LESS SICK

¡IMAGINE! UN MUNDO DONDE HAYA MENOS HAMBRE, MENOS MISERIA, MENOS SOLEDAD, MENOS ENFERMEDADES

IMAGINEZ UN MONDE MOINS AFFAME, MOINS PAUVRE, MOINS SEUL, MOINS MALADE

In the same way that world peace edges nearer when one person extends a hand in friendship, Rotarians understand that small steps create inroads into places where poverty, disease, and hardship are the tragic norm.

De la misma manera que la paz mundial se acerca cuando una persona tiende a otra la mano en señal de amistad, los rotarios creen que son los pequeños pasos los que ayudan a mejorar la situación de sitios en los cuales son trágicamente habituales la miseria, las enfermedades, y todo tipo de penurias.

De même que l'objectif de paix dans le monde se rapproche lorsque quelqu'un tend la main en signe d'amitié, les Rotariens comprennent que de petits pas permettent des incursions dans des endroits où la misère, la maladie et les épreuves sont de tragiques lieux communs.

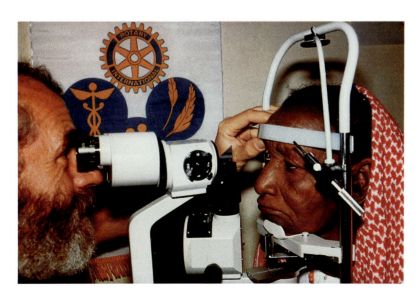

From its early days, Rotary has emphasized the obligation of each individual to change the world for the better. This ideal of service extends beyond the performance of good deeds. It springs from an ability to identify with those who suffer or whose resources are limited.

Desde sus primeros años de existencia, Rotary ha puesto énfasis en la obligación de cada individuo de mejorar el mundo. Este ideal de servicio no se limita al cumplimiento de buenas obras, sino que deriva de la capacidad para identificarse con aquellos que sufren, o cuyos recursos son muy limitados.

Depuis ses débuts, le Rotary a insisté sur l'obligation qu'a chaque personne d'essayer de changer le monde. Cet idéal de service va au-delà de l'accomplissement de bonnes actions. Il naît d'une identification avec ceux qui souffrent et dont les ressources sont limitées.

Rotarians see themselves as agents of change. Working as individuals, within their own Rotary clubs, with other clubs and with other organizations, they look for ways to make life better for neighbors within their communities and in far distant places.

Los rotarios se ven a sí mismos como agentes del cambio. Trabajando a nivel individual, dentros de sus propios Clubes Rotarios, con otros clubes y otras organizaciones, buscan las formas de lograr una vida mejor para los vecinos de sus comunidades y de otros sitios más lejanos.

Les Rotariens se considèrent comme des agents du changement. Travaillant comme personne, au sein de leurs propres Rotary clubs, avec d'autres clubs et d'autres organisations, ils cherchent des moyens d'améliorer les conditions de vie de leurs voisins dans leur ville et dans le monde.

International service opportunities take Rotarians into developing countries to share their resources and expertise. Often bringing dramatic change to places they visit, Rotarians offer time, money, knowledge, and labor to help people improve their own lives.

Through various initiatives of Rotary International, The Rotary Foundation, and individual clubs, Rotarians feed the hungry and help increase agricultural and food production . . .

Las oportunidades de servicio internacional llevan a los rotarios a países en desarrollo a fin de aportar allí sus recursos y experiencia. Los rotarios ofrecen tiempo, dinero, conocimientos y arduo trabajo, para ayudar a mejorar las condiciones de vida de sus semejantes; a menudo los resultados de su esfuerzo son impresionantes.

A través de las diversas iniciativas de Rotary International, La Fundación Rotaria y los propios clubes, los rotarios contribuyen a la alimentación de quienes sufren hambre y al aumento de la producción agrícola y alimentaria . . .

Dans le cadre des programmes internationaux, des Rotariens ont la possibilité de faire bénéficier des communautés de pays en voie de développement de leurs expériences et qualifications. Instaurant souvent des changements bénéfiques là où ils se rendent, les Rotariens offrent leur temps, leurs connaissances et de l'argent pour aider les gens à vivre mieux.

Par le biais de différentes initiatives du Rotary International, de la Fondation Rotary, et de clubs, les Rotariens nourrissent ceux souffrant de malnutrition et accroissent la production agricole . . .

bring water sources to remote
villages . . .

llevan el agua a remotas
aldeas . . .

installent des points d'eau dans
des villages éloignés . . .

teach skills that promote
self-sufficiency . . .

ofrecen enseñanza destinada
a promover la autosu-
ficiencia . . .

enseignent des techniques
diverses pour aboutir à l'auto-
assistance . . .

help with vocational training
and unemployment . . .

ayudan a desarrollar la
formación profesional y el
empleo . . .

offrent des formations professionnelles pour lutter contre le
chômage . . .

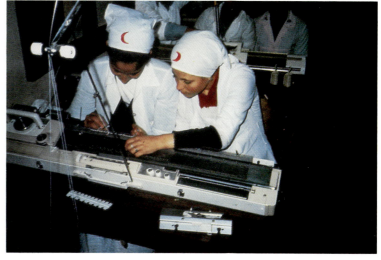

respond to famines, floods and other disasters . . .   brindan ayuda en casos de hambre y carestía; inundaciones y otros desastres . . .   font face aux famines, inondations et catastrophes naturelles . . .

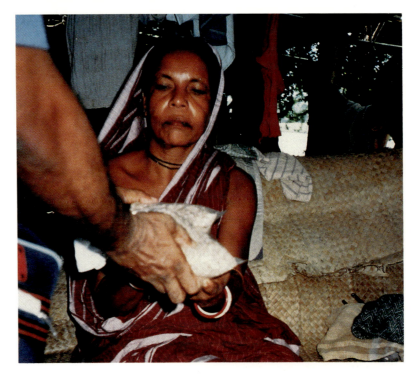

34

improve literacy . . .

combaten el analfabetismo . . .

luttent contre l'illettrisme . . .

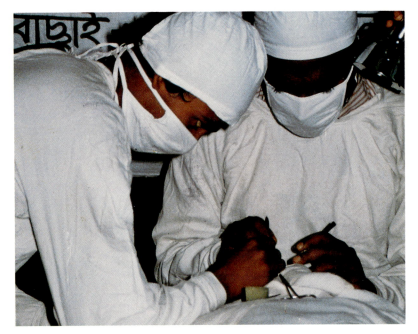

provide medicine,
preserve eyesight, and
prevent disease.

ofrecen atención médica,
preservan la vista y evitan las
enfermedades.

fournissent des médicaments,
restaurent la vue et offrent des
mesures préventives contre la
maladie.

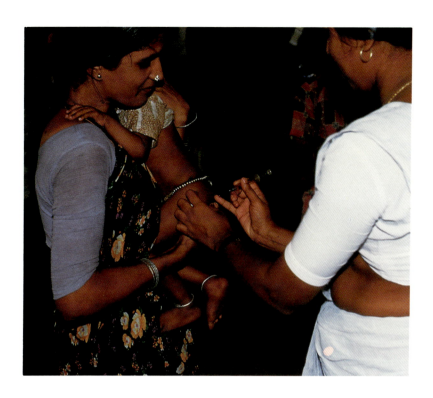

Other forms of service are of a quieter, yet no less dramatic nature. It is often simple things that make life better.

Ejercen también sus actividades de servicio de otras maneras menos espectaculares, pero no menos importantes. A menudo, son las cosas más simples las que contribuyen a una vida mejor.

D'autres formes de service sont d'une nature moins spectaculaire. Ce sont souvent les actions simples qui ont un impact majeur sur les conditions de vie.

40

And so within their own communities, Rotarians construct playgrounds, take children on outings and visit the elderly . . .

A nivel de sus propias comunidades, los rotarios instalan parques infantiles, llevan de excursión a niños y visitan a los ancianos . . .

Et donc dans leurs propres communautés, les Rotariens construisent des terrains de jeux, organisent des sorties pour les enfants et rendent visite à des personnes âgées . . .

41

sponsor sports events,
camps and special activities
for disabled people . . .

42

auspician eventos deportivos, campamentos y actividades especiales para las personas impedidas . . .

parrainent des rencontres sportives, des camps et activités spéciales pour handicapés . . .

restore historical sites . . .
plant public gardens . . .
clean up roadsides . . .

restauran sitios históricos . . .
plantan jardines públicos . . .
limpian carreteras y sitios
aledaños . . .

restaurent des sites
historiques . . .
reboisent des jardins
publics . . .
nettoient les bas-côtés de
routes . . .

raise funds for community
services . . .
sponsor health clinics . . .
donate blood . . .

recaudan fondos para servicios
a la comunidad . . .
patrocinan dispensarios médicos . . .
donan sangre . . .

collectent des fonds pour des
actions d'intérêt public . . .
parrainent des centres
sanitaires . . .
donnent du sang . . .

gather clothing . . .
collect books . . .
solicit surplus supplies . . .

donan indumentaria . . .
donan libros . . .
solicitan mercancía de saldo
para donar . . .

rassemblent des vêtements, des
livres, cherchent des fournitures en surplus . . .
s'occupent de personnes
seules . . .

befriend the lonely . . .
build hostels for students . . .
teach people to read . . .
develop job skills . . .

dan su amistad a los
solitarios . . .
construyen albergues
estudiantiles . . .
enseñan a la gente a leer . . .
capacitan a la gente para en-
contrar trabajo . . .

construisent des cités univer-
sitaires . . .
apprennent à lire à certains . . .
développent les qualifications
professionnelles d'autres . . .

With their vision fixed on a better world, Rotarians go wherever they see a need to be served. They offer to do or to give whatever they can.

Guided by their motto, "Service Above Self," they teach . . .

En virtud de su visión de un mundo mejor, los rotarios van dondequiera que sus servicios hagan falta. Se ofrecen para realizar o donar todo lo que esté a su alcance.

Inspirándose en su lema "Dar de sí antes de pensar en sí", enseñan . . .

Rêvant d'un monde meilleur, les Rotariens vont partout où ils voient un besoin auquel il faut répondre. Ils offrent de faire tout ce qui est en leur pouvoir.

Guidés par leur devise, "Servir d'abord", ils enseignent . . .

build . . .
feed . . .
comfort . . .
and heal.

construyen . . .
brindan alimentación . . .
ayudan . . .
y curan.

construisent . . .
nourrissent . . .
réconfortent . . .
et soignent.

49

WHO COULD HAVE IMAGINED!
¡QUIEN SE HUBIERA IMAGINADO!
QUI L'AURAIT IMAGINÉ !

Attorney Paul Harris, right, laid the foundation for what was to become an international organization of more than one million men and women when he formed a club with Chicago colleagues Hiram Shorey, a merchant tailor, Silvester Schiele, a coal dealer, and Gustavus Loehr, a mining engineer.

Al formar un club en Chicago junto a sus colegas Hiram Shorey (sastre), Silvester Schiele (comerciante en carbón) y Gustavus Loehr (ingeniero de minas), el abogado Paul Harris (derecha), sentó las bases de lo que se convertiría en el futuro, en una organización internacional de más de un millón de hombres y mujeres.

L'avocat Paul Harris, à droite, a posé les fondations de ce qui allait devenir une organisation internationale de plus d'un million d'hommes et de femmes lorsqu'il forma un club avec ses collègues Hiram Shorey, tailleur, Silvester Schiele, marchand de charbon, et Gustavus Loehr, ingénieur des mines.

Rotary began in 1905 when a man named Paul Harris gathered three colleagues together in a quest for camaraderie. The initiative came from his longing to recreate in the bewildering city of Chicago the small-town friendliness and sense of belonging he had experienced growing up in New England.

Today, more than 1.1 million people are members of 25,000-plus Rotary clubs around the world. Apparently others have felt the same desire to belong to a small, significant community within a larger universe.

Paul Harris was often asked whether he ever imagined that his idea would reach such proportions. "No, I did not in 1905 foresee a worldwide movement. . . . When a man plants an unpromising sapling in the early springtime, can he be sure that someday here will grow a mighty tree? Does he not have to reckon with the rain and sun—and the smile of Providence? Once he sees the first bud—ah, then he can begin to dream of shade."

Rotary fue fundado en 1905, cuando en cierta ocasión un hombre llamado Paul Harris se reunió con tres colegas a los efectos de fomentar la camaradería. Esta iniciativa tuvo origen en su anhelo de recrear en la desconcertante ciudad de Chicago, la amistad y el sentimiento de pertenencia que había experimentado durante su niñez en un pueblecito de Nueva Inglaterra.

Hoy Rotary cuenta con más de 1,1 millones de socios, pertenecientes a más de 25.000 Clubes Rotarios de todo el mundo. Resulta evidente que eran muchos los que compartían dicho anhelo de pertenecer a una pequeña y significativa comunidad ubicada dentro de un universo mucho más amplio.

Se le solía preguntar a Paul Harris si en aquel entonces se le había ocurrido que su idea llegaría a alcanzar tales proporciones. "No, en 1905 ese tipo de predicción estaba fuera de mi alcance . . . Cuando un hombre planta un humilde arbusto a comienzos de la primavera, ¿cómo podría estar seguro de que algún día llegará a ser un poderoso árbol? ¿No tiene acaso que contar con la lluvia, el sol . . . y la Providencia? Una vez que despunta el primer brote . . . ya se puede empezar a soñar con la sombra que dará el árbol".

Le Rotary naquit de l'initiative d'un homme du nom de Paul Harris. Poussé par le désir ardent de recréer dans la ville déconcertante de Chicago l'atmosphère amicale et conviviale qu'il avait connue durant son enfance dans un village de la Nouvelle Angleterre, il décida de réunir trois de ses collègues en vue d'encourager la camaraderie.

Aujourd'hui, le Rotary compte plus de 1,1 million de membres répartis dans quelque 25.000 clubs de par le monde. Il est apparent que d'autres ressentirent ce même besoin d'appartenir à une communauté, petite mais significative, au sein d'un univers beaucoup plus vaste.

On a souvent demandé à Paul Harris s'il avait jamais imaginé que son idée prendrait de telles proportions. "Non. En 1905, je ne concevais pas un mouvement international . . . Lorsqu'un homme plante un jeune arbre incertain au début du printemps, peut-il être sûr qu'un jour il grandira pour devenir un arbre plein de vigueur ? Ne doit-il pas compter avec la pluie et le soleil et la Providence ? Une fois le premier bourgeon éclos, alors il peut commencer à rêver d'ombre."

The sapling did flourish, surviving the furies of wars, bending to the winds of cultural change—growing steadily in size and stature. Core principles that were present at its founding are still central to the organization and embraced by people in more than 170 countries and geographical areas. It is those values that best define Rotary International today.

El arbusto rotario floreció, sobreviviendo a la furia de varias guerras, adaptándose a las corrientes del cambio cultural, creciendo firmemente y adquiriendo superior categoría. Los principios fundamentales de aquellos primeros tiempos configuran aún la base de la organización y son aceptados por personas de más de 170 países y regiones geográficas. Son precisamente esos valores los que mejor definen a Rotary International en la actualidad.

Le jeune plant fleurit, échappant aux furies de la guerre, s'adaptant au vent des changements culturels, grandissant sûrement. Les principes fondamentaux de ces premières années constituent toujours les fondements de cette organisation, adoptés par des habitants de plus de 170 pays et régions. Ce sont précisément ces valeurs qui définissent le mieux le Rotary International dans son actualité.

Rotary has survived dramatic changes in many parts of the world. At one time, Rotary was so prominent in Czechoslovakia that the organization's European Advisory Committee met there. Later, Rotary clubs disappeared from Eastern European countries as a result of World War II and Communist takeovers after the war. At the end of the 1980s, however, the return of democratic freedoms to those countries brought with it the rechartering of once vital Rotary clubs.

Rotary ha sobrevivido a dramáticos cambios en diversos sitios del mundo. Debido a la gran prominencia alcanzada por Rotary en Checoeslovaquia en determinada época, se decidió que en dicho país estuviera la sede del Comité Consultivo para Europa. Debido a la Segunda Guerra Mundial y a la toma del poder por los comunistas, desaparecieron los Clubes Rotarios de Europa Oriental. A finales de la década de 1980, la restauración de las libertades democráticas en tales naciones trajo consigo un nuevo otorgamiento de cartas constitutivas a Clubes Rotarios que, en el pasado, habían alcanzado una importancia fundamental.

Le Rotary a survécu à des changements considérables dans de nombreuses parties du monde. Dans le passé, le Rotary était si prédominant en Tchécoslovaquie que la commission consultative européenne du Rotary s'y réunissait. Plus tard, les Rotary clubs ont disparu des pays d'Europe de l'Est à la suite de la Seconde guerre mondiale et de l'emprise communiste. A la fin des années 80 néanmoins, le retour des libertés démocratiques dans ces pays a apporté avec lui la reconstitution de Rotary clubs, autrefois essentiels.

The adventurous spirit of Paul Harris, shown here on a goodwill trip to Japan, fostered respect for other cultures that remains a core principle of Rotary International.

El espíritu abierto de Paul Harris, plenamente demostrado en ocasión de este viaje de buena voluntad al Japón, fomentó el respeto a otras culturas, principio que Rotary International siempre ha mantenido.

L'esprit aventureux de Paul Harris, visible ici dans un voyage de bonne volonté au Japon, encouragea le respect pour d'autres cultures qui reste un principe au coeur du Rotary International.

While he missed the nurturing familiarity of small-town life, Paul Harris was also intrigued and fascinated by the wider world. As a young man, he was curious about other people's lives and spent five years "vagabonding," as he put it, living in different places and trying out different types of work. Experiencing both a sense of loneliness among strangers and the warm hospitality extended by some of them, he believed that finding opportunities for people to get to know one another would help them discover

Aunque extrañaba la familiaridad de la vida de su comarca, Paul Harris se sentía también fascinado e intrigado por el ancho mundo exterior a tales fronteras. Cuando joven, sentía curiosidad sobre la vida de otra gente, y pasó cinco años "vagabundeando", como solía él mismo expresar, viviendo en diferentes sitios y probando diversos tipos de trabajo. Al haber experimentado tanto la soledad de encontrarse entre extraños como la cálida hospitalidad que personas desconocidas le ofrecían, llegó a la conclusión de que hacía falta crear oportunidades para que la gente de todas partes se co-

Bien que la convivialité des petites villes lui ait manqué, Paul Harris était néanmoins fasciné par le monde qui s'étendait au delà de ces frontières. Jeune, il s'enquérait de ce que pouvait être la vie dans d'autres contrées, et il passa cinq années à "vagabonder" selon ses propres termes, vivant dans des régions diverses, et essayant plusieurs métiers. Ressentant parfois un sentiment de solitude parmi ses hôtes et une chaleureuse hospitalité chez d'autres, il en vint à penser que si l'occasion était offerte aux jeunes de mieux se connaître, ils pourraient découvrir leurs

commonalities and lay a foundation for friendship.

Today, Rotary International celebrates its diversity and emphasizes educational and service programs that enable people to experience and understand another's circumstances. People of different countries, cultures, lifestyles, ages, races, and vocations overcome their estrangement by learning how much they have in common.

nozca, descubriendo en tal proceso sus características comunes y creando una firme base para la amistad.

En la actualidad, Rotary International celebra su diversidad, enfatizando asimismo los programas educativos y de servicio que permiten a los seres humanos experimentar y comprender las circunstancias en que viven los demás. Personas de diversos países, culturas, estilos de vida, edades, orígenes raciales y profesiones, superan las barreras que las separan, enterándose de los puntos que tienen en común.

points communs et créer les bases solides d'une amitié.

Aujourd'hui, le Rotary International se fait joie de sa diversité et concentre son action sur des programmes éducatifs et de service qui permettent aux gens de découvrir et de comprendre d'autres cultures. Des gens de divers pays, race, profession et âge vainquent les barrières qui les séparent en apprenant combien ils ont en commun.

Paul Harris believed that the idea of Rotary would appeal to people from many different countries and cultures. Here, he is shown being received by the Lord Provost of Edinburgh, Scotland, in 1934.

Paul Harris creía que el concepto de Rotary podría atraer a gente de diferentes países y culturas. Vemos aquí al fundador, recibido por Lord Provost de Edinburgh, Escocia, en 1934.

Paul Harris croyait que l'idée du Rotary serait appréciée par des gens de différentes cultures et pays. On le voit ici reçu par Lord Provost d'Edinburgh en 1934.

Another important principle that Paul Harris upheld was the spirit of helping. Again drawing on his early years, he sought to recreate a community in which people knew each other's problems and needs, and offered what they could to make things better. In addition to the fellowship it provided, that first Rotary club in Chicago was a forum for addressing the problems of young, struggling businessmen.

The service mission came to the fore in the organization's earliest years, when Rotarians from different parts of the United States joined to help victims of a Midwestern flood. Today, Rotary International stands as the forerunner and archetype of what have come to be known as service clubs. Each local Rotary Club and each Rotarian is challenged to look for ways to be of service to others. Service takes many forms as Rotarians reach out to a single individual in need, throw their collective support behind a community project, or help people in developing countries improve their lives.

Otro importante principio sustentado por Paul Harris fue el espíritu de ayuda. Nuevamente, inspirándose en sus años de juventud, intentó recrear una comunidad en la cual sus integrantes conociesen los problemas y las necesidades de los demás, ofreciendo todo el apoyo posible para mejorar su situación. Además del compañerismo brindado, aquel primer Club Rotario de Chicago constituyó un foro para tratar los problemas de sus jóvenes y emprendedores hombres de negocios.

La misión de servicio adquirió relieve durante los primeros años de la organización, cuando los rotarios de diversos sitios de los Estados Unidos unieron sus fuerzas para ayudar a las víctimas de una inundación en el Medio Oeste de dicha nación. Hoy, Rotary International es considerado como arquetipo y precursor de las entidades conocidas mundialmente como clubes de servicio. Cada uno de los Clubes Rotarios de cada localidad y cada uno de los rotarios hacen frente al desafío de intentar brindar servicio a los demás de todas las maneras posibles. El servicio adopta diversas formas, a medida que los rotarios tienden su mano a un individuo necesitado, otorgan su apoyo colectivo a un proyecto de ayuda a la comunidad, o ayudan a la población de los países en desarrollo a mejorar sus condiciones de vida.

L'esprit d'entraide est un autre principe inspiré par Paul Harris. Au début de sa carrière, il s'efforça de recréer une communauté où les habitants s'enquerraient des besoins d'autrui et offriraient leur aide. En plus de l'atmosphère de camaraderie que le premier Rotary club offrait, il constituait un forum où l'on traitait des problèmes des jeunes hommes d'affaires débutants.

La mission de service se dessina dans les premières années d'existence du Rotary, lorsque les Rotariens de plusieurs états des Etats-Unis s'unirent pour aider les victimes d'une inondation dans le Middle West.

Le Rotary est de nos jours considéré comme un précurseur et un archétype de ce que sont maintenant les clubs de service. Chaque Rotary club et Rotarien est mis au défi de trouver des occasions d'aider autrui. Le service peut revêtir diverses formes, que ce soit pour assister une personne dans le besoin, soutenir un projet au bénéfice de toute la communauté ou essayer d'améliorer les conditions de vie d'habitants d'un pays moins avancé.

Sensitive to the suffering of others, Rotary clubs came to the aid of those in strife-torn Europe at the end of World War II.

Demostrando su solidaridad con el sufrimiento de los demás, los Clubes Rotarios brindaron su generosa ayuda a los pobladores del devastado continente europeo, a fines de la Segunda Guerra Mundial.

Sensibles à la souffrance des autres, les Rotary clubs sont venus au secours de ceux qui vivaient dans une Europe déchirée à la fin de la Seconde Guerre mondiale.

From the early days, Rotarians knew how to have fun. After this "Society Circus" outing in 1913, townspeople labeled these members of the Rotary Club of Chicago as slightly "crack-brained."

Desde los primeros días, los rotarios han sabido divertirse. Tras esta excursión de la "Sociedad Circense" en 1913, los residentes de la ciudad empezaron a creer que los socios del Club Rotario de Chicago estaban un poco "mal de la chaveta".

Dès les premières années, les Rotariens ont su s'amuser. Après cette sortie "Société du Cirque" en 1913, les gens attribuèrent aux membres du Rotary club de Chicago le qualificatif: un peu "timbrés".

Early in its history, Rotary earned the reputation for being onto something. After both World Wars I and II and to this day, groups such as the United Nations have called upon the organization to help bring about global understanding, taking note of Rotary's bent toward peace and the role model it has become for others.

Throughout its growth and expansion, the local club has remained the lifeblood of Rotary. It is within the intimacy of that which is familiar that people learn to enjoy and help one another. Thus grounded, Rotarians then venture out into the unfamiliar to do these same things.

A comienzos de su historia, Rotary se ganó la justa reputación de estar realizando obras significativas. Con posterioridad a las dos guerras mundiales y hasta la fecha, entidades tales como las Naciones Unidas han convocado a la organización a fomentar la comprensión global, teniendo en cuenta la inclinación de Rotary a favor de la paz y el magnífico ejemplo que constituye para los demás.

A través de su crecimiento y expansión, la verdadera savia de Rotary ha seguido siendo el club de cada localidad. Dicho marco familiar es ideal para que la gente aprenda a divertirse y ayudarse mutuamente. Una vez consolidado este punto de partida, los rotarios pueden aventurarse y realizar su positiva gestión en un medio menos familiar.

The camaraderie and friendship of the local club were important elements of the first Rotary clubs, as they continue to be today.

La camaradería y la amistad del club de la localidad fueron elementos de suma importancia para los primeros Clubes Rotarios, y lo siguen siendo.

La camaraderie et l'amitié dans les clubs représentaient un élément important des premiers Rotary clubs, comme c'est toujours le cas aujourd'hui.

Au début de son histoire, le Rotary gagna la réputation de précurseur. Après les deux guerres mondiales, et jusqu'à nos jours, des organismes tels que les Nations Unies ont fait appel au Rotary pour encourager l'entente mondiale, connaissant son attachement à la paix et l'exemple qu'il constitue pour les autres à cet égard.

Au cours de sa croissance et de son expansion, le club local est resté le pivot du Rotary. Ce domaine familier est idéal pour que les gens apprennent à s'apprécier et à s'entraider. Une fois ce point de départ bien établi, les Rotariens peuvent s'aventurer à en faire de même dans un environnement moins familier.

There is one area where Paul Harris's vision fell short of what could be. In sync with his times, when he built his forum of friends from among his colleagues in the business community, he spoke only of a men's club. He probably could not have imagined a time when women would lead local businesses or hold professional positions. But the world changed, and so did Rotary, when in 1989 all Rotary clubs were permitted to admit women into membership.

Paul Harris may not have imagined it, but, in a sense, he foretold it when he spoke of the inclusive nature of Rotary's platform, which is "broad enough to include all sorts of people as long as they are friendly, tolerant and unselfish."

Hay un área en la cual la visión de Paul Harris no llegó a anticiparse a futuros acontecimientos. El foro por él creado de amigos pertenecientes a la comunidad empresarial, a tono con la época, configuró un club de cuadro social enteramente masculino. Seguramente no había podido imaginarse que llegaría el día en el cual las mujeres iban también a dirigir empresas u ocupar cargos profesionales. No obstante, grandes cambios iban a producirse en el mundo y en Rotary: en 1989 se autorizó a todos los Clubes Rotarios a admitir mujeres en su cuadro social.

Paul Harris no podría haberlo imaginado pero, en cierto sentido, supo predecir tal evolución al referirse a la naturaleza global de Rotary, entidad "suficientemente amplia como para admitir a toda clase de personas, siempre y cuando sean amigables, tolerantes y altruístas".

Il existe un domaine où Paul Harris ne sut anticiper les événements futurs. Le forum d'amis du milieu des affaires qu'il créa était, en accord avec son temps, un club uniquement composé d'hommes. Paul Harris ne pouvait sans doute pas imaginer que le jour viendrait où les femmes seraient à la tête d'entreprises ou épouseraient des professions libérales. Mais de grands changements devaient surgir dans le monde et au Rotary. En 1989 tous les Rotary clubs furent autorisés à accepter des femmes parmi leurs rangs.

Même si Paul Harris n'avait pas envisagé un tel futur, ses propres mots au regard de la nature globale du Rotary — une entité suffisamment vaste pour inclure toutes sortes d'êtres tant qu'ils sont amicaux, tolérants et altruistes — en avaient certainement présagé la possibilité.

The assortment of headgear worn by members of this early "reception committee" may have given rise to the persistent rumor that Rotarians "wear funny hats."

La gran variedad de sombreros de los integrantes de este antiguo "Comité de Recepción" puede haber sido el motivo que dio lugar al persistente rumor de que los rotarios "tenían la cabeza en todo".

L'assortiment de couvre-chefs portés par les membres de ce "comité de réception" des tous débuts a peut-être causé la rumeur persistante que les Rotariens "portent des chapeaux curieux".

CATCHING THE WORLD'S IMAGINATION

MOTIVANDO LA IMAGINACION DEL MUNDO

LE MONDE SAISI D'IMAGINATION

Just before the Berlin wall was dismantled in 1989, someone scrawled the word "Rotary" across it in large letters. The meaning of that anonymous act was seen by some as the triumph of freedom, which Rotary exemplifies, over the repression and separateness symbolized by the wall.

Poco antes de que fuese desmantelado el muro de Berlín en 1989, alguien garabateó sobre uno de sus sectores la palabra "Rotary" en grandes caracteres. Hubo quienes vieron en dicho acto anónimo el triunfo de la libertad, valor que Rotary tan dignamente representa, sobre el estado de represión y aislamiento simbolizado por el muro.

Juste avant la chute du mur de Berlin, un inconnu y grava le mot "Rotary" en larges lettres. Cet acte anonyme fut perçu par certains comme l'expression de la liberté, que le Rotary personnifie, triomphant de l'état de répression et de séparation symbolisé par le mur.

62

Because of the simple principles and universal values the organization has upheld since its founding, the very word "Rotary" carries implicit messages wherever it is heard or seen.

Debido a los sencillos principios y valores universales preconizados por la organización, dondequiera que se lo perciba, el término "Rotary" lleva implícito el mensaje que lo caracteriza.

En raison des principes simples et des valeurs universelles adoptés par l'organisation depuis sa création, le mot même de "Rotary" est porteur de messages implicites partout où il est entendu ou vu.

Outside cities and villages throughout the world, the familiar gear wheel emblem stands as testimony that Rotary is at work there and that the local community is linked to a larger universe.

Sobre la entrada de pueblos y ciudades de todo el mundo, el conocido emblema de la rueda dentada da a entender que Rotary está presente con su labor, nexo de unión entre cada comunidad y un universo mucho más amplio.

A l'entrée de villes et villages de par le monde, l'emblème bien connu de la roue dentée témoigne que le Rotary est à l'oeuvre et que la communauté locale est liée à un monde plus vaste.

Through the years, Rotary has formed bonds with a host of world leaders, celebrities, and prominent people who have joined its ranks, participated in its programs, embodied its values, benefited from its service, or been inspired by its dreams.

A través de los años, Rotary ha creado vínculos con gran cantidad de líderes mundiales, celebridades y personas de gran prominencia que se han sumado a sus filas, han participado en sus programas, aceptado sus valores, han cosechado los beneficios del servicio brindado por la entidad, o han recibido la inspiración de sus sueños.

Au cours des ans, le Rotary a tissé des liens avec des dirigeants mondiaux, des célébrités et des personnes influentes qui ont joint ses rangs, participé et bénéficié de ses programmes, adopté ses valeurs, ou qui ont été inspirés par ses rêves.

Prime Minister Margaret Thatcher of Great Britain, daughter of a Rotary club president, in 1990 became an honorary Rotarian herself at the invitation of a London club.

La primera ministra de Gran Bretaña Margaret Thatcher, cuyo padre fuera presidente de un Club Rotario, adquirió la condición de rotaria honoraria en virtud de la invitación de un club de Londres.

Le Premier ministre de Grande Bretagne, Margaret Thatcher, fille d'un président de Rotary club, devint membre d'honneur sur invitation d'un club de Londres.

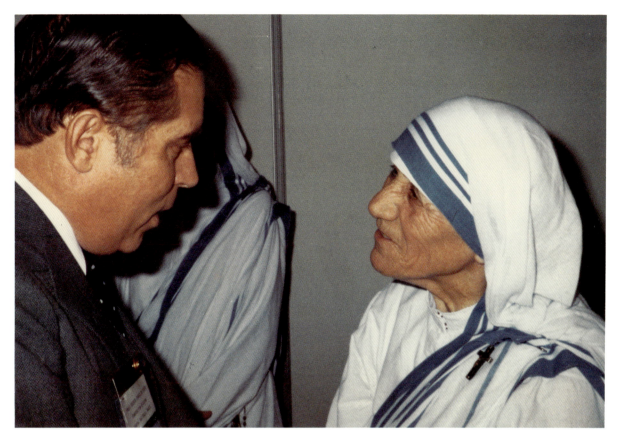

R.I. President Paulo Costa and Mother Teresa share a common vision of peace through service.

El Presidente de RI Paulo Costa y la Madre Teresa comparten la misma visión en pro de la causa de la paz, mediante el servicio al prójimo.

Le Président du RI Paulo Costa et Mère Teresa partagent l'idée de la paix dans le service à autrui.

Dr. L.M. Singhvi of India's Supreme Court was a Rotary Foundation graduate scholar in 1953-54.

El Dr. L.M. Singhvi, integrante de la Suprema Corte de la India, fue becario de La Fundación Rotaria.

Le Docteur L.M. Singhvi de la Cour Suprême d'Inde était un boursier de la Fondation Rotary.

During Ronald Reagan's term as U.S. president, the Reagans and then Vice President and Mrs. George Bush welcomed recipients of Rotary's Gift of Life project to the White House in Washington, D.C.

Durante la presidencia de Ronald Reagan en los EEUU, el primer mandatario y su esposa, junto al entonces vicepresidente George Bush y su cónyuge, dieron la bienvenida a la Casa Blanca a los beneficiarios del proyecto "Gift of Life".

Durant le mandat de Ronald Reagan en tant que président des Etats-Unis, Monsieur et Madame Reagan ainsi que le vice-président d'alors, George Bush et son épouse, ont reçu à la maison blanche les récipiendaires du projet du Rotary "Gift of Life".

Thailand's Porntip "Kuhn" Narkhirunkanok helped promote Rotary's PolioPlus project during her reign as Miss Universe.

Porntip "Kuhn" Narkhirunkanok ayudó a promover el programa PolioPlus de Rotary, durante su reinado como Miss Universo.

Porntip "Kuhn" Narkhirunkanok a aidé à la promotion des projets PolioPlus du Rotary durant son règne de Miss Univers.

Irish Republic President Mary Robinson praised the work of Rotary for strengthening bonds of friendship between Ireland's two states.

La presidenta de la República de Irlanda Mary Robinson elogió la labor de Rotary en pro del fortalecimiento de los lazos de amistad entre los dos estados irlandeses en conflicto.

Le Président de la République d'Irlande, Mary Robinson, a fait l' éloge du travail du Rotary visant à renforcer les liens d'amitié entre les deux états d'Irlande.

71

When Rotary initiates a program or embraces an issue, the impact of that support is significant. A prime example of Rotary's influence can be seen in its massive undertaking to rid the world of polio and other childhood diseases through the PolioPlus program. Begun in 1985, this ambitious effort captured the interest not only of Rotarians, but also of international bodies, governments, health organizations, and the general public.

Cuando Rotary emprende un programa o decide dedicarse a determinada cuestión, el impacto de dicho apoyo resulta altamente significativo. Uno de los mejores ejemplos de la influencia rotaria puede apreciarse al considerar su masivo empeño para liberar al mundo de la polio y otras enfermedades de la niñez mediante el programa PolioPlus. Iniciado en 1985, este ambicioso empeño concitó el interés no sólo de los rotarios sino también de organismos internacionales, gobiernos, organizaciones de la salud y el público en general.

Chaque fois que le Rotary lance un programme ou prend sous son aile un problème spécifique, l'impact de cette action est considérable. Un exemple précis de cette influence peut être vu dans l'engagement massif du Rotary pour éliminer de la surface de la terre la poliomyélite et d'autres maladies infantiles au travers du programme PolioPlus. Cette action ambitieuse, initiée en 1985, a captivé non seulement les Rotariens, mais aussi des organismes internationaux, des gouvernements, des organisations sanitaires et le public.

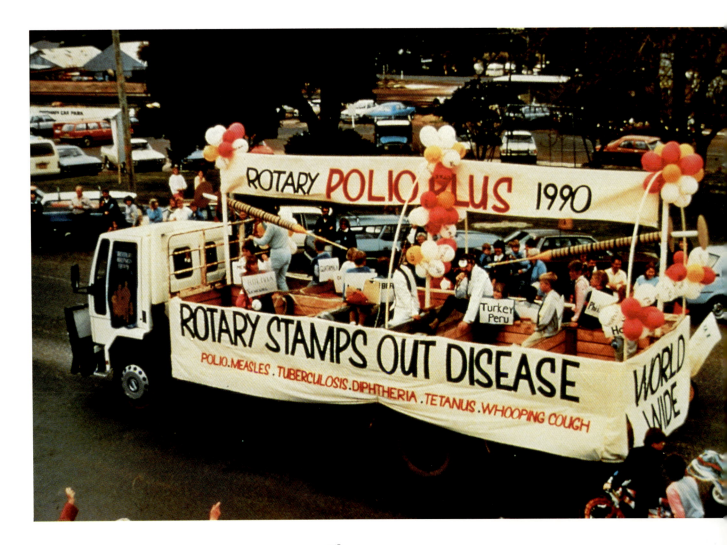

This dream took more than imagination. It took leadership to work within the many different systems, cultures, and bureaucracies that would be crucial to success in nearly 100 developing countries. It took commitment, determination, organization, and hard work. And it took money. Early in the fundraising campaign, Rotarians set a goal of $120 million. Five years later, nearly twice that amount had been raised.

Para este sueño hizo falta
más que imaginación. Fue necesario contar con un liderazgo capaz de trabajar en
diferentes sistemas, culturas y
andamiajes burocráticos; factor fundamental para lograr el
éxito en casi 100 países en desarrollo. Fue necesario el com-
promiso, la decisión, la organización, y la denodada labor de
los participantes. También
hizo falta dinero. Al principio
de la campaña, los rotarios se
fijaron como meta recaudar
120 millones de dólares. Cinco
años después se había logrado
recaudar casi el doble de dicha
cantidad.

Ce rêve a nécessité bien
plus que de l'imagination pour
être réalisé. Il a requis une attitude de leader pour travailler
avec divers systèmes, cultures,
et bureaucraties. Attitude qui
devait s'avérer cruciale pour
exécuter les projets dans quelque cent pays en voie de développement. Cela a requis de
l'engagement, de la détermination, de l'organisation et beaucoup de travail. Et de l'argent.
Tout au début de la campagne,
les Rotariens s'étaient fixé le
but de 120 millions de dollars.
Cinq ans plus tard, presque le
double de ce montant était col-
lecté.

The PolioPlus story was primarily about putting substance to a vision. It demonstrated Rotary's ability to effect major change by marshalling its unique strength and influence. That strength comes not merely from the sheer size of the organization or its international dimensions, but from its ability to mobilize a multifaceted membership into a unified force for good.

La historia de PolioPlus fue fundamentalmente llevar a la realidad una visión. Demostró a las claras la capacidad de Rotary para lograr positivos cambios, canalizando debidamente su singular fortaleza e influencia. Tal fortaleza no es el fruto de la enorme cantidad de socios y clubes, ni de su dimensión internacional, sino de su capacidad para movilizar a su diverso cuadro social, integrando un cuerpo unitario de fuerzas para el bien.

L'histoire de PolioPlus consistait en fait à insuffler de la substance à un rêve. Elle a montré que le Rotary était capable d'instaurer des changements majeurs en mettant à l'oeuvre sa force et son influence. Cette force ne vient pas simplement de la taille de l'organisation ou de son caractère international, mais de sa capacité à mobiliser un effectif varié pour en faire une force unie pour le bien.

As a result of PolioPlus, more than 500 million children will be protected from the ravages of this disease and eventually, polio will be a part of the past.

Como consecuencia del éxito de PolioPlus, más de 500 millones de niños han sido inmunizados contra los estragos de dicha enfermedad y se da ya por descontado que la polio pronto será un problema del pasado.

Grâce à PolioPlus, plus de cinq cents millions d'enfants seront protégés des ravages de la poliomyélite, et cette maladie fera bientôt partie du passé.

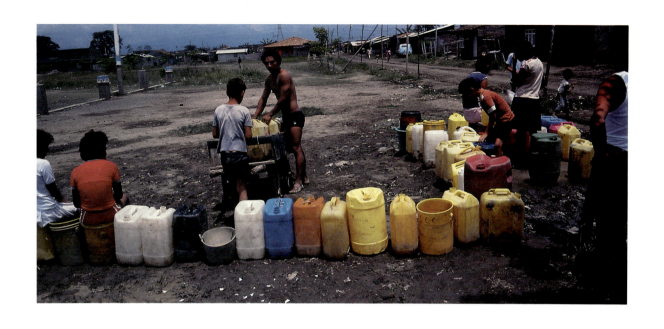

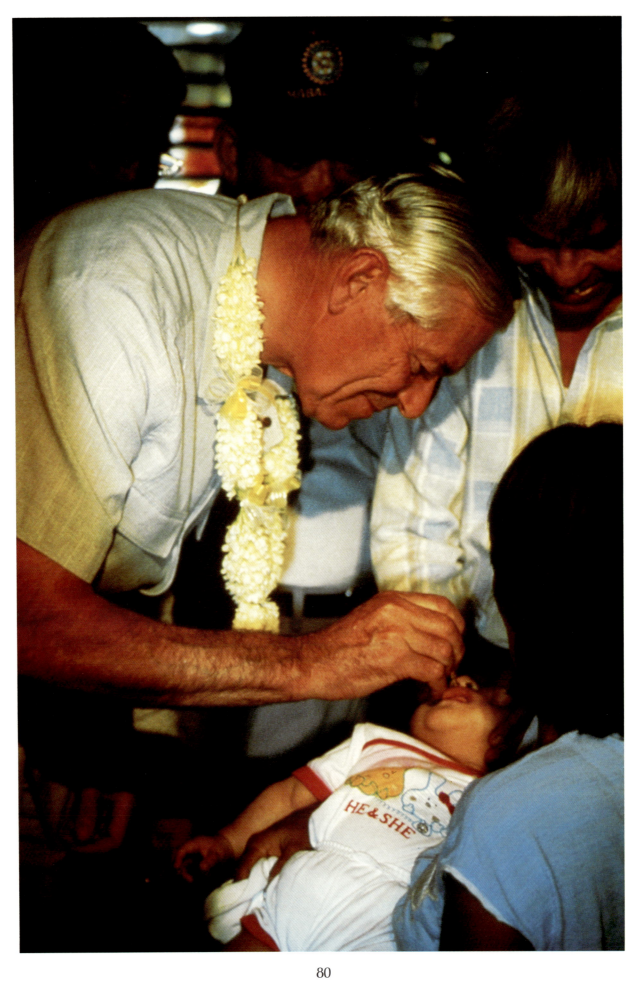

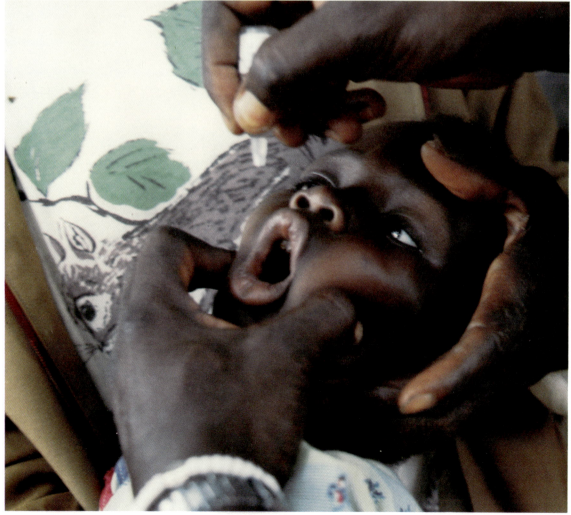

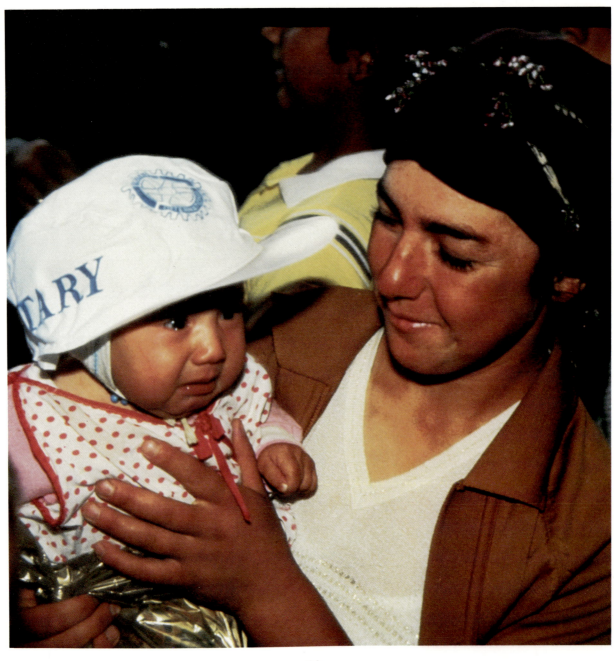

82

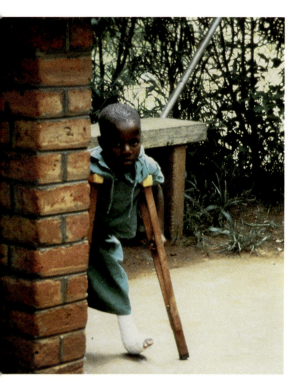

Altering the status quo and ensuring that the future will be better is the focus of another ambitious Rotary goal to Preserve Planet Earth. Introduced in 1990, the program was developed in recognition of the world's limited physical resources and the responsibility of the planet's citizens to care for it.

La modificación de las adversas circunstancias ecológicas actuales y asegurar un futuro mucho mejor es el objetivo de otro ambicioso programa de Rotary, conocido como Preservemos el Planeta Tierra. Este programa, emprendido en 1990, tiene su origen en el reconocimiento de la tremenda limitación de los recursos naturales del planeta y la responsabilidad de protegerlo que compete a los seres humanos que en él habitan.

Conscient des limitations de nos ressources naturelles, le Rotary International a introduit en 1990 le programme intitulé "Protégeons notre planète" afin d'assurer un avenir meilleur pour les prochaines générations et d'initier une prise de conscience générale du besoin de sauvegarder notre planète.

The tree-planting tradition goes back to Rotary's founder Paul Harris, who promoted the planting of "friendship trees" between nations.

La tradición de plantar árboles data de la época del fundador Paul Harris, quien promovió la plantación de "árboles de amistad".

La tradition de planter des arbres remonte au Fondateur du Rotary Paul Harris, qui a promu la plantation "d'arbres de l'amitié".

84

A través de los Clubes Rotarios de sus respectivas localidades, los rotarios han dado inicio a proyectos destinados a plantar cientos de millones de árboles. Jóvenes y ancianos, personas comunes y corrientes y famosos líderes han sabido ponerse a tono con el espíritu de Preservemos el Planeta Tierra plantando semilleros en diversos sitios.

Au travers de leurs clubs, les Rotariens ont lancé des projets qui permettront que des milliers d'arbres soient plantés. Jeunes et moins jeunes, citoyens ordinaires et dirigeants célèbres ont souscrit à l'esprit de protection de la planète, plantant des semis ici et là.

Through their local clubs, Rotarians have initiated projects that will result in the planting of hundreds of millions of trees. Young and old, average citizens and famous leaders have caught the spirit of Preserve Planet Earth by planting a variety of seedlings in a variety of settings.

91

Preserve Planet Earth has also inspired cleanup projects, recycling campaigns, solar energy exploration, wildlife preservation efforts, and research and education programs. Rotarians continue to seek innovative ways to be guardians and preservers of this planet—our only home.

Preservemos el Planeta Tierra también ha dado lugar a proyectos de limpieza, campañas de reciclado, proyectos de preservación de especies amenazadas, programas de investigación y educación. Los rotarios siguen buscando renovadoras maneras para constituirse en los custodios de este planeta, defendiendo así nuestro único hogar.

Le programme de sauvegarde de la terre a également inspiré des projets d'épuration et de nettoiement, des campagnes de recyclage, une exploration plus poussée de l'énergie solaire, des activités de protection de la nature et de la vie sauvage, et des programmes de recherche et d'éducation. Les Rotariens continuent d'explorer des moyens innovateurs pour préserver cette planète qui est notre seul habitat.

94

IMAGINE WHAT THE FUTURE WILL BE!

¡IMAGINEMOS LO QUE PODRIA SER EL FUTURO!

IMAGINEZ LE FUTUR!

In Japan, the display of festive carp streamers symbolizes the hope of parents that their children will grow up with the courage and vitality of this colorful fish, known for its ability to ascend waterfalls.

En el Japón, el Festival Infantil, con sus coloridos estandartes de carpas de colores, simboliza la esperanza de los padres de que sus hijos crezcan y adquieran el coraje y la vitalidad de este colorido pez, conocido por su tremenda capacidad para remontar saltos de agua.

Au Japon, les banderoles représentant une espèce de carpes symbolisent pour les parents l'espoir que leurs enfants grandiront possédant le courage et la vitalité de ce poisson coloré, connu pour son habilité à remonter les cours d'eau.

With similar hopes and dreams for their offspring, Rotarians everywhere recognize that the world's future depends on its children.

Con similares esperanzas y sueños para sus descendientes, los rotarios de todas partes reconocen que el futuro del mundo depende de la niñez.

Baignés d'espoirs et de rêves similaires, les Rotariens reconnaissent de concert que l'avenir du monde dépend des enfants.

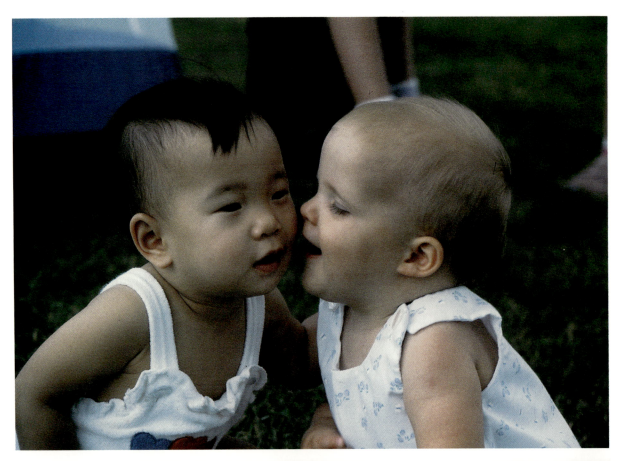

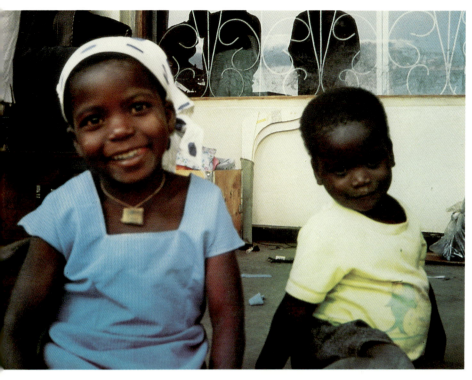

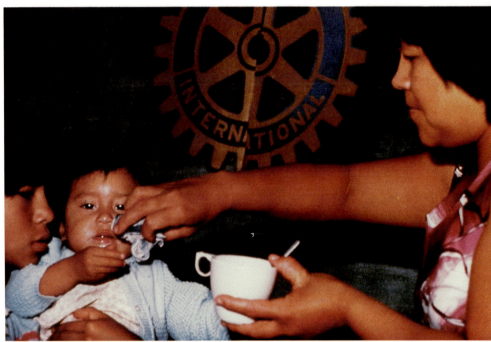

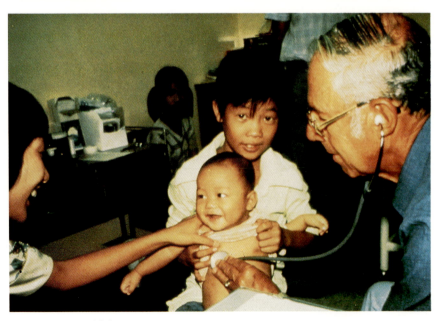

The nurturing of the next generation takes place on many fronts within Rotary, beginning with the provision of basic care for those children who are without food, shelter, and medicine. Through programs of The Rotary Foundation, Rotary International and local club initiatives, Rotarians teach children to read, provide equipment that helps them learn and discover, immunize them against life-threatening diseases, pay for surgeries that save lives, inspire them to resist drug use, distribute surplus food and clothing, and in dozens of other ways help them to survive and grow.

La formación de la próxima generación tiene lugar en diversos frentes dentro de Rotary, comenzando por la provisión de atención básica para aquellos niños que carecen de alimentación, vivienda, y servicios médicos. A través de los programas de La Fundación Rotaria, Rotary International, e iniciativas a cargo de los clubes, los rotarios enseñan a los niños a leer, les proporcionan equipo para ayudarlos a aprender y descubrir, los inmunizan contra mortales enfermedades, sufragan los costos de intervenciones quirúrgicas necesarias para salvarles la vida, los inspiran para resistir al influjo de la drogadicción, obtienen para ellos lotes de saldos de alimentación e indumentaria, y de muchas otras formas los ayudan a sobrevivir y crecer.

L'éducation de la prochaine génération s'organise sur de nombreux fronts au sein du Rotary, en commençant par fournir des soins primaires aux enfants auxquels font défaut nourriture, foyer, et médicaments. Grâce aux programmes de la Fondation Rotary, du Rotary International et des clubs, les Rotariens enseignent la lecture et l'écriture aux enfants. Ils leur offrent du matériel leur permettant d'apprendre et de comprendre, les immunisent contre des maladies mortelles, assument les frais de chirurgies salutaires, les aident à résister à la tentation des drogues, leur distribuent de la nourriture et des vêtements, et les assistent de dizaines d'autres manières pour qu'ils grandissent dans des conditions meilleures.

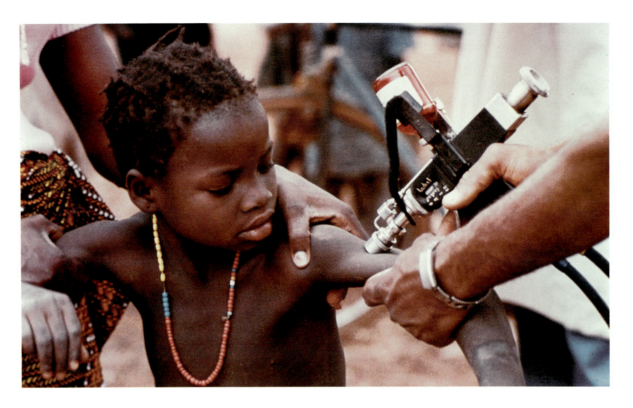

Rotarians also know that children need to play and experience childhood as carefree and joyous. Many local clubs take youngsters on outings, sponsor camps and sports events, share hobbies or simply spend time getting to know them. Opportunities for teaching and influence are plentiful in these settings, enabling adults to pass on values as well as knowledge to succeeding generations.

108

Los rotarios son también conscientes de que los niños tienen derecho a jugar y disfrutar una niñez alegre y sin preocupaciones. Numerosos clubes de diversas localidades llevan de excursión a los chicos, auspician campamentos y actividades deportivas, comparten con ellos sus pasatiempos, o sencillamente dedican tiempo a conversar con los niños. En tales contextos, abundan las oportunidades para enseñar y ejercer influencia, permitiendo a los adultos trasmitir valores y conocimientos a las generaciones venideras.

Les Rotariens savent également que les enfants ont besoin de jouer et qu'ils devraient pouvoir se souvenir de leur enfance comme d'une époque insouciante et joyeuse. De nombreux membres de clubs accompagnent des jeunes dans des sorties, parrainent des camps et des événements sportifs, partagent leur passion avec eux ou s'attachent tout simplement à mieux les connaître. Les occasions d'enseigner ou d'aider abondent et permettent aux adultes de passer leurs valeurs et leurs connaissances à la génération suivante.

110

113

Because the world of work has always been central to the makeup of Rotary membership in the local club, career guidance is a natural area of shared interest through which Rotarians support the transition into adulthood. Rotarians offer tours of their work sites, sponsor career fairs, and speak to groups of young people to help them discover satisfying vocations. Rotary clubs help foster leadership ability through such programs as the Rotary Youth Leadership Awards (RYLA), designed to recognize and train those who will become tomorrow's leaders.

115

Dado que el mundo del trabajo siempre ha ocupado un sitio prominente para la integración del cuadro social de los clubes, la orientación sobre carreras es un aspecto a través del cual los rotarios pueden ayudar a los adolescentes a superar los escollos que vivan en su transición hacia la edad adulta. Los rotarios organizan visitas guiadas a sus lugares de trabajo, auspician jornadas de orientación vocacional, y pronuncian alocuciones ante grupos de jóvenes ayudándolos a descubrir profesiones que les sean satisfactorias. Los Clubes Rotarios fomentan su capacidad de liderazgo a través de programas tales como los Seminarios de Rotary para Líderes Jóvenes (RYLA), destinados a reconocer y capacitar debidamente a los líderes del mañana.

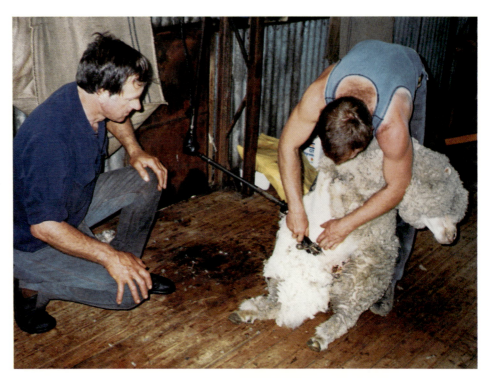

Parce que le monde du travail a toujours été primordial dans la constitution de l'effectif du club rotarien, l'orientation professionnelle est un centre d'intérêt que les Rotariens partagent avec les jeunes, tout en rendant la transition vers l'âge adulte plus aisée. Ils offrent des visites de leur lieu de travail, organisent des foires aux carrières et font des présentations à des groupes de jeunes pour les aider à découvrir des professions enrichissantes. Les Rotary clubs encouragent le développement des qualités de leader par le biais des Activités rotariennes pour la promotion de la jeunesse (RYLA en anglais), conçues pour identifier puis former ceux qui deviendront les dirigeants de demain.

116

117

118

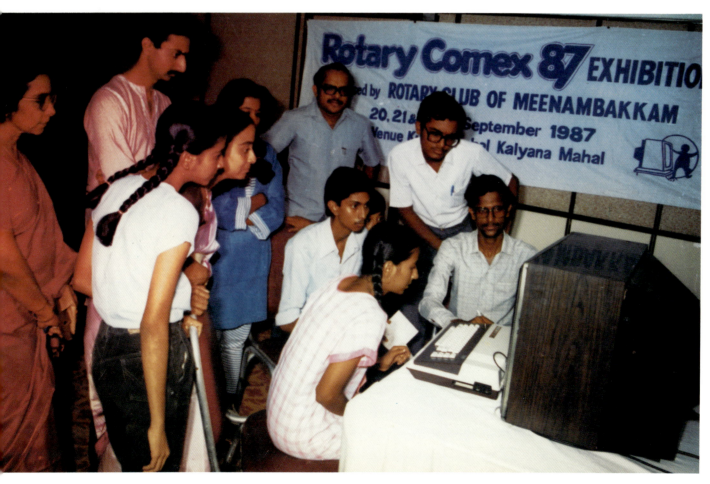

Another important principle that Rotarians strive to share with youth is their belief in the importance of getting to know and understand people from other nations. For nearly 70 years, Rotary clubs have been sponsoring visits of young people to other countries. Today, about 10,000 Youth Exchange visits occur each year. Sponsored by their home club, these teenagers are welcomed into the home of a Rotarian in the host country where they experience life as a member of that family.

Otro de los importantes principios que los rotarios anhelan compartir con la juventud es la importancia de conocer y comprender a la gente de otras naciones. Durante casi 70 años, los Clubes Rotarios han estado patrocinando visitas de jóvenes a otros países. En la actualidad, se efectúan aproximadamente 10.000 visitas de Intercambio de Jóvenes al año. Bajo los auspicios del Club Rotario de sus respectivas localidades, estos adolescentes son hospedados en hogares de familias rotarias de los países anfitriones, en donde experimentan el modo de vida de tales familias.

L'autre principe fondamental que les Rotariens s'efforcent de partager avec les jeunes est l'importance d'apprendre, de connaître et de comprendre les populations étrangères. Depuis presque 70 ans, les clubs rotariens parrainent des visites de jeunes gens vers d'autres pays. Actuellement, quelque 10.000 échanges de jeunes s'effectuent par an. Patronnés par leur club local, ces adolescents sont accueillis chez des Rotariens du pays hôte où ils vivent comme un membre de la famille. Dans le cadre de son remarquable

123

Through its outstanding scholarship program, The Rotary Foundation also has enabled thousands of young adults to spend a year of study in a country other than their own, broadening their formal education as well as their understanding of another culture and people. In the process, the scholars also serve as goodwill ambassadors.

A través de su destacado programa de Becas de Buena Voluntad, La Fundación Rotaria ha dado también oportunidad a miles de jóvenes adultos a cursar un año de estudios fuera de su propio país, ampliando no sólo su educación académica sino también su comprensión de otros pueblos y culturas. En dicho proceso los becarios sirven también como embajadores de buena voluntad.

programme de bourses d'études, la Fondation Rotary a également permis à des milliers de jeunes adultes de passer une année d'études dans un pays étranger, parfaisant leur éducation en même temps que leur compréhension d'une autre culture et d'un autre peuple. Les boursiers servent simultanément d'ambassadeurs de bonne volonté.

124

126

127

But perhaps the most important principle that Rotarians instill in the next generation is the ideal of service to others. Through Interact clubs, for youth between the ages of 14-18, and Rotaract, for young adults ages 18-29, young people work together under the sponsorship of a local Rotary club to support humanitarian causes in their own communities and abroad.

No obstante, el principio de mayor importancia que los rotarios pueden inculcar a la nueva generación es el ideal del servicio a los demás. A través de los Clubes Interact, para jóvenes con edades comprendidas entre 14 y 18 años, y Rotaract, para jóvenes adultos con edades comprendidas entre 18 y 29 años, se da ocasión a la juventud de trabajar mancomunadamente a nivel local, bajo el patrocinio de un Club Rotario, brindando apoyo a causas humanitarias en sus propias comunidades y fuera de fronteras.

Mais peut-être le principe le plus important que les Rotariens essaient d'instiller à la prochaine génération réside-t-il dans l'idéal de servir autrui. Grâce aux clubs Interact, destinés aux quatorze/dix-huit ans, et aux clubs Rotaract pour les dix-huit/vingt-neuf ans, des jeunes travaillent ensemble sous le parrainage d'un Rotary club local pour soutenir des causes humanitaires dans leur communauté ou à l'étranger.

132

133

In service to and with the children, youth, and young adults who will carry on their traditions and values, Rotarians forge a link with the future and help determine what that future will be.

Mediante el servicio a la niñez y con la niñez, a los jóvenes y jóvenes adultos destinados a heredar sus tradiciones y valores, los rotarios forjan un firme vínculo de cara al futuro, ayudando asimismo a configurar la orientación de dicho futuro.

En aidant les enfants, les adolescents et les jeunes adultes, qui perpétueront leurs traditions et valeurs, les Rotariens tissent un lien avec le futur et contribuent ainsi à le façonner.

134

135

THOSE IMAGINATIVE ROTARIANS

LOS IMAGINATIVOS ROTARIOS

DES ROTARIENS PLEINS D'IMAGINATION

Who are these Rotarians? Does the stereotype of a stodgy, humorless man in a business suit represent the true image of Rotary?

¿Quiénes son los rotarios? ¿Puede decirse que el estereotipo de un trajeado y robusto insulso hombre de negocios es la verdadera imagen de Rotary?

Qui sont ces Rotariens ? Le stéréotype de l'homme d'affaires gauche et sans humour correspond-il à la véritable image du Rotary ?

For the official portrait of Rotary's founder, the painter depicted a serious Paul Harris.

Para este retrato oficial del fundador de Rotary, el pintor retrató a un Paul Harris de rostro serio.

Pour le portrait officiel du fondateur du Rotary, l'artiste a dépeint un Paul Harris austère.

Not exactly.   Verdaderamente, no.   Pas exactement.

But as this pose suggests, Paul Har-   *¡Pero, como sugiere la imagen, Paul*   *Mais, comme le suggère la photo, Paul*
ris was no stuffed shirt!   *Harris no era nada pretencioso!*   *Harris n'était pas prétentieux!*

Rotary clubs throughout the world are still composed of leaders drawn from the local business and professional community. Being invited into membership in Rotary is deemed a privilege, bestowed with honor on those who take the responsibility seriously.

Los Clubes Rotarios del mundo entero están integrados por destacados líderes de la comunidad empresarial y profesional de cada localidad. Ser invitado a asociarse a Rotary se considera un privilegio, otorgado con todos los honores a quienes asuman seriamente tal responsabilidad.

Les clubs rotariens de par le monde sont composés de chefs de file issus du monde des affaires et des professions libérales de leur communauté. Etre invité à joindre le Rotary est considéré comme un privilège accordé avec honneur à ceux qui assument cette responsabilité avec sérieux.

But Rotarians are not all men, they don't all wear business suits, and most are not afraid to enjoy themselves as they serve their communities.

No todas las personas socias de Rotary son hombres, ni necesariamente visten traje, y en su mayor parte no tienen reparo en divertirse mientras sirven a sus comunidades.

Mais les membres du Rotary ne sont pas tous des hommes, ils ne portent pas tous des costumes, et la plupart d'entre eux n'ont pas peur de s'amuser tout en servant leur communauté.

143

Among Rotary club ranks are people who are willing to risk and to dream. They are people who live life to the fullest and know that such joys as kite flying are not just for children. Rotarians challenge themselves and try new things. They are adventuresome, fun-loving, creative, and energetic.

Rotary cuenta en sus filas con gente dispuesta a correr riesgos y soñar; gente que aprovecha la vida al máximo y bien sabe que placeres tales como remontar cometas no están sólo reservados a los niños. Los rotarios se plantean el reto de intentar cosas nuevas. Poseen asimismo un enorme caudal de energía y creatividad, no temen tampoco a las innovaciones y les gusta divertirse.

Dans les rangs du Rotary se trouvent des gens prêts à prendre des risques et prêts à rêver. Ce sont des gens qui vivent pleinement et qui savent que les cerfs-volants ne sont pas uniquement faits pour les enfants. Ils se lancent des défis et aiment innover. Ils sont aventureux, créatifs, pleins d'entrain et d'énergie.

147

Their innovative spirit often surfaces in the fund-raising activities they sponsor to support service projects. Whether it is the traditional Rotary pancake day, an elaborate telethon fund-raising event, or one of the zany races or competitions they are capable of dreaming up, Rotarians have a good time on their way to doing good work.

Su espíritu renovador se trasluce con frecuencia en las actividades de recaudación de fondos destinadas a la financiación de proyectos de servicio, se trate de actividades como el tradicional y sencillo día rotario de los *pancakes,* un complejo *telemaratón* destinado a obtener fondos, o las originales carreras y competencias que se atreven a imaginar, los rotarios pasan momentos sumamente agradables mientras realizan su positiva obra.

Leur esprit d'innovation fait souvent surface lors des campagnes de collecte de fonds qu'ils parrainent pour soutenir des projets de service. Que ce soit un téléthon ou une course loufoque, ils s'amusent sur la route qui mène vers le bien.

150

151

But imagination involves more than being childlike and playful. It requires a willingness to take on challenges and to see beyond the obvious. Imagination is grounded in hope. It is this belief in what could be—this sense of imagination—that inspires Rotarians to ask:

"Is it possible to bring water to this desert?"

"Is it possible to eliminate a devastating disease?"

"Can we save this child's life . . . help this man support his family . . . build this dam . . . renew this forest?"

Claro está que el alcance de la imaginación no se limita a jugar con espíritu juvenil. Requiere también una firme disposición de aceptar desafíos y ver más allá de lo obvio. La imaginación se basa en la esperanza. Es precisamente esta creencia en lo que podría realizarse el factor que inspira a los rotarios a plantearse preguntas tales como: "¿es posible eliminar una enfermedad devastadora?"; "¿está a nuestro alcance salvar la vida de un niño, ayudar a un hombre a mantener a su familia, construir un embalse o repoblar una arboleda?"

Mais il ne suffit pas d'être enfantin et joueur pour être imaginatif. Cela nécessite la volonté d'accepter des défis et de voir au-delà de l'évident. L'imagination est fondée sur l'espoir. C'est la croyance en ce qui pourrait être — ce sentiment d'imagination — qui inspire les Rotariens à demander : "Est-il possible d'amener l'eau jusqu'à ce désert ?" ou "Est-il possible d'éliminer une maladie dévastatrice ?" ou encore "Peut-on sauver la vie d'un enfant, aider cet homme à subvenir aux besoins de sa famille, construire un barrage, reboiser une région ?"

154

155

Rotarians believe that if they can conceive of something, they can work to make it so. Though they are widely recognized for the work they do, they know that vision comes first. It is a truth set forth by founder Paul Harris in his autobiography:

"There were moments while indulging myself in daydreams on the mountainside when my conscience rebuked me for not being up and doing; so many things needed to be done in this busy world and there was so little time in which to do them, and then the thought came to me that perhaps men had to dream. . . ."

Los rotarios creen que si la concepción de una idea es posible, está a su alcance la posibilidad de llevarla a la práctica. Aunque se les reconoce ampliamente por la labor que cumplen, saben muy bien que en primer lugar hace falta crear una visión. Como muy bien supo expresar el fundador Paul Harris en su autobiografía:

"Hubo momentos en los cuales me he permitido soñar despierto en las montañas, y me remordió la conciencia por no estar haciendo nada; hacía falta hacer tantas cosas en este ajetreado mundo y el tiempo disponible era sumamente escaso; pero luego me puse a pensar en que quizá fuese necesario que la gente se atreviese a soñar".

Les Rotariens pensent que s'ils peuvent concevoir un projet, alors ils ont le pouvoir d'en faire une réalité. Bien que leurs actions soient largement reconnues, ils savent que derrière tout projet mené à terme se cache un rêve. C'est une vérité que le fondateur Paul Harris a établie dans son autobiographie :

"Il y avait des moments où, m'abandonnant à la rêverie au pied d'une montagne, ma conscience me réprimandait car je n'étais pas debout à agir ; tant de choses avaient besoin d'être accomplies dans ce monde agité et il y avait si peu de temps. Puis la pensée m'est venue que peut-être les hommes devaient rêver . . . "

THE CONVENTIONS OF ROTARY INTERNATIONAL

1910	Chicago, Illinois, U.S.A.		1951	Atlantic City, New Jersey, U.S.A.
1911	Portland, Oregon, U.S.A.		1952	Mexico City, Mexico
1912	Duluth, Minnesota, U.S.A.		1953	Paris, France
1913	Buffalo, New York, U.S.A.		1954	Seattle, Washington, U.S.A.
1914	Houston, Texas, U.S.A.		1955	Chicago, Illinois, U.S.A.
1915	San Francisco, California, U.S.A.		1956	Philadelphia, Pennsylvania, U.S.A.
1916	Cincinnati, Ohio, U.S.A.		1957	Lucerne, Switzerland
1917	Atlanta, Georgia, U.S.A.		1958	Dallas, Texas, U.S.A.
1918	Kansas City, Missouri, U.S.A.		1959	New York, New York, U.S.A.
1919	Salt Lake City, Utah, U.S.A.		1960	Miami-Miami Beach, Florida, U.S.A.
1920	Atlantic City, New Jersey, U.S.A.		1961	Tokyo, Japan
1921	Edinburgh, Scotland		1962	Los Angeles, California, U.S.A.
1922	Los Angeles, California, U.S.A.		1963	St. Louis, Missouri, U.S.A.
1923	St. Louis, Missouri, U.S.A.		1964	Toronto, Ontario, Canada
1924	Toronto, Ontario, Canada		1965	Atlantic City, New Jersey, U.S.A.
1925	Cleveland, Ohio, U.S.A.		1966	Denver, Colorado, U.S.A.
1926	Denver, Colorado, U.S.A.		1967	Nice, France
1927	Oostende, Belgium		1968	Mexico City, Mexico
1928	Minneapolis, Minnesota, U.S.A.		1969	Honolulu, Hawaii, U.S.A.
1929	Dallas, Texas, U.S.A.		1970	Atlanta, Georgia, U.S.A.
1930	Chicago, Illinois, U.S.A.		1971	Sydney, New South Wales, Australia
1931	Vienna, Austria		1972	Houston, Texas, U.S.A.
1932	Seattle, Washington, U.S.A.		1973	Lausanne, Switzerland
1933	Boston, Massachusetts, U.S.A.		1974	Minneapolis-St. Paul, Minnesota U.S.A.
1934	Detroit, Michigan, U.S.A.		1975	Montreal, Quebec, Canada
1935	Mexico City, Mexico		1976	New Orleans, Louisiana, U.S.A.
1936	Atlantic City, New Jersey, U.S.A.		1977	San Francisco, California, U.S.A.
1937	Nice, France		1978	Tokyo, Japan
1938	San Francisco, California, U.S.A.		1979	Rome, Italy
1939	Cleveland, Ohio, U.S.A.		1980	Chicago, Illinois, U.S.A.
1940	Havana, Cuba		1981	Sao Paulo, Brazil
1941	Denver, Colorado, U.S.A.		1982	Dallas, Texas, U.S.A.
1942	Toronto, Ontario, Canada		1983	Toronto, Ontario, Canada
1943	St. Louis, Missouri, U.S.A.		1984	Birmingham, England
1944	Chicago, Illinois, U.S.A.		1985	Kansas City, Missouri, U.S.A.
1945	Chicago, Illinois, U.S.A.		1986	Las Vegas, Nevada, U.S.A.
1946	Atlantic City, New Jersey, U.S.A.		1987	Munich, Germany
1947	San Francisco, California, U.S.A.		1988	Philadelphia, Pennsylvania, U.S.A.
1948	Rio de Janeiro, Brazil		1989	Seoul, Korea
1949	New York, New York, U.S.A.		1990	Portland, Oregon, U.S.A.
1950	Detroit, Michigan, U.S.A.		1991	Mexico City, Mexico

134

135
132 94
91 72
76
161
152
168
166
158
153
162
160
167
156
155
157
163
165
172
77
133
75
93
171
128
100
108
120
164 154
170
159
169
141
143
148 151 139
150 142
144
149
140
146
145
69 105
99 104
125
130
116

N
W E
S

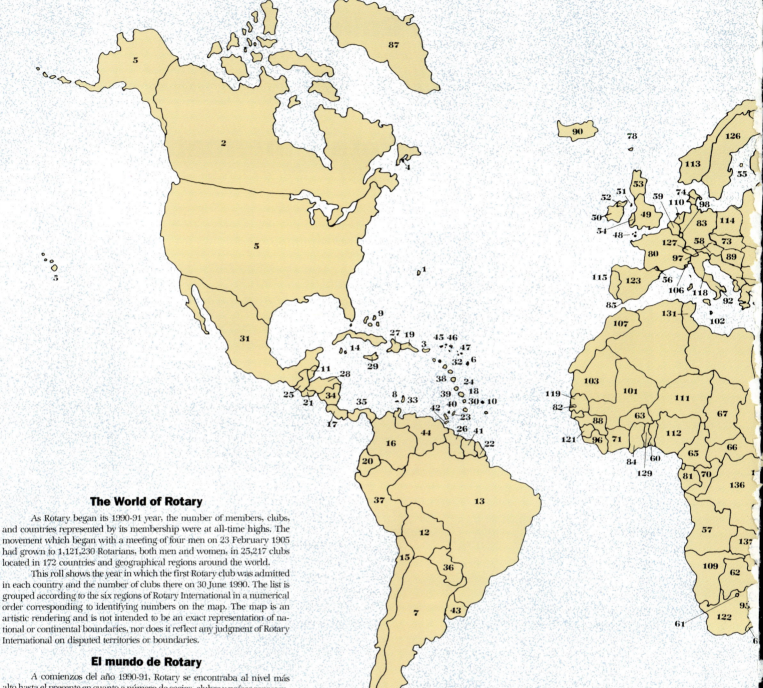

The World of Rotary

As Rotary began its 1990-91 year, the number of members, clubs, and countries represented by its membership were at all-time highs. The movement which began with a meeting of four men on 23 February 1905 had grown to 1,121,230 Rotarians, both men and women, in 25,217 clubs located in 172 countries and geographical regions around the world.

This roll shows the year in which the first Rotary club was admitted in each country and the number of clubs there on 30 June 1990. The list is grouped according to the six regions of Rotary International in a numerical order corresponding to identifying numbers on the map. The map is an artistic rendering and is not intended to be an exact representation of national or continental boundaries, nor does it reflect any judgment of Rotary International on disputed territories or boundaries.

El mundo de Rotary

A comienzos del año 1990-91, Rotary se encontraba al nivel más alto hasta el presente en cuanto a número de socios, clubes y países representados en la organización. El movimiento, iniciado el 23 de febrero de 1905, con una reunión a la que asistieron cuatro hombres, había alcanzado la cifra de 1.121.230 rotarios —hombres y mujeres— afiliados a 25.217 clubes ubicados en 172 países y regiones geográficas de todo el mundo.

Esta lista muestra el año en que el primer Club Rotario de cada país fue admitido en RI y el número de clubes existentes en tales naciones al 30 de junio de 1990. En dicha lista, elaborada agrupando a los países según las seis regiones de Rotary International, los mismos son identificados siguiendo un orden numérico que corresponde a los números que figuran en el mapa. Este es un mapa de carácter artístico que no pretende representar con exactitud las fronteras nacionales o continentales, ni refleja la opinión de Rotary International sobre fronteras o territorios en disputa.

Le monde du Rotary

Au début de l'année rotarienne 1990-91, le Rotary comptait un nombre inégalé de membres et pays représentés. Le mouvement, qui débuta avec la réunion de quatre hommes le 23 février 1905, est aujourd'hui constitué de 1.121.230 membres, hommes et femmes, répartis dans 172 pays et régions.

Ces colonnes montrent l'année de création du premier Rotary club de chaque pays et le nombre de clubs présents au 30 juin 1990. La liste est organisée selon les six régions du Rotary International et est classée par ordre numérique correspondant aux numéros sur la carte. Cette carte est une représentation artistique et ne se propose pas de refléter de manière exacte les frontières nationales ou continentales, ni un jugement quelconque du Rotary International relatif à des conflits frontaliers ou territoriaux.

United States, Canada, and Bermuda

1. Bermuda (1924) 4
2. Canada (1910) 592
3. Puerto Rico (1918) 48
4. St. Pierre & Miquelon (1989) 1
5. U.S.A. (1905) 7,141

South America, Central America, Mexico, Antilles

6. Antigua & Barbuda (1972) 1
7. Argentina (1920) 628
8. Aruba (1938) 1
9. Bahamas (1962) 9
10. Barbados (1962) 3
11. Belize (1957) 3
12. Bolivia (1927) 29
13. Brazil (1923) 1,703
14. Cayman Islands (1965) 3
15. Chile (1924) 217
16. Colombia (1927) 133
17. Costa Rica (1927) 14
18. Dominica (1973) 1
19. Dominican Republic (1943) 48
20. Ecuador (1927) 36
21. El Salvador (1927) 8
22. French Guiana (1958) 3

23. Grenada (1968) 2
24. Guadeloupe (1957) 8
25. Guatemala (1925) 15
26. Guyana (1959) 4
27. Haiti (1962) 7
28. Honduras (1929) 20
29. Jamaica (1959) 16
30. Martinique (1957) 6
31. Mexico (1921) 554
32. Montserrat (1970) 1
33. Netherlands Antilles (1937) 4
34. Nicaragua (1929) 10
35. Panama (1919) 8
36. Paraguay (1928) 22
37. Peru (1922) 118
38. St. Kitts-Nevis (1969) 1
39. St. Lucia (1966) 2
40. St. Vincent & Grenadines (1966) 2
41. Suriname (1953) 2
42. Trinidad & Tobago (1957) 14
43. Uruguay (1919) 103
44. Venezuela (1937) 98
45. Virgin Islands (Brit.) (1968) 1
46. Virgin Islands (U.S.A.) (1957) 7
47. West Indies Assoc. States (1978) 1

Great Britain and

48. Channel Isla
49. England (19
50. Ireland (191
51. Isle of Man
52. Northern Ire
53. Scotland (19
54. Wales (1917)

Continental Europe Eastern Mediterra

55. Aland Island
56. Andorra (19
57. Angola (195
58. Austria (192
59. Belgium (19
60. Benin (1965)
61. Bophuthatsv
62. Botswana (1
63. Burkina Fas
64. Burundi (19
65. Cameroun (
66. Central Afric
67. Chad (1957)
68. Ciskei (1950
69. Comoro Isla
70. Congo (1958)

A Rotary Portrait Gallery

Personalidades rotarias

Personnalités du Rotary International

Paul P. Harris
U.S.A.
1910-11 and 1911-12

Glenn C. Mead
U.S.A.   1912-13

Russell F. Greiner
U.S.A.   1913-14

Frank L. Mulholland
U.S.A.   1914-15

Allen D. Albert
U.S.A.   1915-16

Arch C. Klumph
U.S.A.   1916-17

E. Leslie Pidgeon
Canada   1917-18

John Poole
U.S.A.   1918-19

Presidents of Rotary International
Presidentes de Rotary International
Présidents du Rotary International

Albert S. Adams
U.S.A.   1919-20

Estes Snedecor
U.S.A.   1920-21

Crawford C. McCullough
Canada   1921-22

Raymond M. Havens
U.S.A.   1922-23

Guy Gundaker
U.S.A.   1923-24

Everett W. Hill
U.S.A.   1924-25

Donald A. Adams
U.S.A.   1925-26

Harry H. Rogers
U.S.A.   1926-27

Arthur H. Sapp
U.S.A.   1927-28

I.B. Tom Sutton
México   1928-29

M. Eugene Newsom
U.S.A.   1929-30

Almon E. Roth
U.S.A.   1930-31

165

Sydney W. Pascall
England   1931-32

Clinton P. Anderson
U.S.A.   1932-33

John Nelson
Canada   1933-34

Robert E. Lee Hill
U.S.A.   1934-35

Ed R. Johnson
U.S.A.   1935-36

Will R. Manier, Jr.
U.S.A.   1936-37

Maurice Duperrey
France   1937-38

George C. Hager
U.S.A.   1938-39

Walter D. Head
U.S.A.   1939-40

Armando
de Arruda Pereira
Brazil   1940-41

Tom J. Davis
U.S.A.   1941-42

Fernando Carbajal
Perú   1942-43

Charles L. Wheeler
U.S.A.   1943-44

Richard H. Wells
U.S.A.   1944-45

T.A. Warren
England   1945-46

Richard C. Hedke
U.S.A.   1946-47

S. Kendrick Guernsey
U.S.A.   1947-48

Angus S. Mitchell
Australia   1948-49

Percy Hodgson
U.S.A.   1949-50

Arthur Lagueux
Canada   1950-51

Frank E. Spain
U.S.A.   1951-52

H.J. Brunnier
U.S.A.   1952-53

Joaquín Serratosa Cibils
Uruguay   1953-54

Herbert J. Taylor
U.S.A.   1954-55

167

A.Z. Baker
U.S.A.   1955-56

Gian Paolo Lang
Italy   1956-57

Charles G. Tennent
U.S.A.   1957-58

Clifford A. Randall
U.S.A.   1958-59

Harold T. Thomas
New Zealand   1959-60

J. Edd McLaughlin
U.S.A.   1960-61

Joseph A. Abey
U.S.A.   1961-62

Nitish C. Laharry
India   1962-63

Carl P. Miller
U.S.A.   1963-64

Charles W. Pettengill
U.S.A.   1964-65

C.P.H. Teenstra
The Netherlands
1965-66

Richard L. Evans
U.S.A.   1966-67

Luther H. Hodges
U.S.A.   1967-68

Kiyoshi Togasaki
Japan   1968-69

James F. Conway
U.S.A.   1969-70

William E. Walk, Jr.
U.S.A.   1970-71

Ernst G. Breitholtz
Sweden   1971-72

Roy D. Hickman
U.S.A.   1972-73

William C. Carter
England   1973-74

William R. Robbins
U.S.A.   1974-75

Ernesto Imbassahy
de Mello
Brazil   1975-76

Robert A. Manchester II
U.S.A.   1976-77

W. Jack Davis
Bermuda   1977-78

Clem Renouf
Australia   1978-79

James L. Bomar, Jr.
U.S.A.   1979-80

Rolf J. Klärich
Finland   1980-81

Stanley E. McCaffrey
U.S.A.   1981-82

Hiroji Mukasa
Japan   1982-83

William E. Skelton
U.S.A.   1983-84

Carlos Canseco
México   1984-85

Edward F. Cadman
U.S.A.   1985-86

M.A.T. Caparas
Philippines   1986-87

Charles C. Keller
U.S.A.   1987-88

Royce Abbey
Australia   1988-89

Hugh M. Archer
U.S.A.   1989-90

Paulo V.C. Costa
Brazil   1990-91

Rajendra K. Saboo
India   1991-92

General Secretaries of Rotary International
Secretarios generales de Rotary International
Secrétaires généraux du Rotary International

Chesley R. Perry
1910-42

Philip Lovejoy
1942-52

George R. Means
1953-72

Harry A. Stewart
1972-78

Herbert A. Pigman
1979-86

Philip H. Lindsey
1986-89

Spencer Robinson, Jr.
1990-

Recipients of the Rotary International Award for World Understanding

Personas agraciadas con el Premio de Rotary pro Comprensión Mundial

Récipiendaires du Prix de l'entente mondiale du Rotary International

Dr. Noboru Iwamura, Japan
Doctor to the Poor of Nepal—1981

Dr. Noboru Iwamura, Japón,
médico de los pobres, Nepal —1981

Dr. Noboru Iwamura, Japon
Médecin auprès des déshérités du
Népal—1981

Pope John Paul II—1982

El Papa Juan Pablo II —1982

Le Pape Jean Paul II—1982

Dr. Lotta Hitschmanova, Canada Founding Director, Unitarian Service Committee—1983

Dra. Lotta Hitschmanova, Canadá, directora fundadora, Comité Unitario de Servicio —1983

Dr. Lotta Hitschmanova, Canada Directrice et fondatrice du Comité unitarien de service—1983

World Organization of the Scout Movement—1984

Organización Mundial del Movimiento Scout —1984

L'Organisation mondiale de Scoutisme—1984

Dr. Albert Sabin, U.S.A. Developer of Oral Polio Vaccine— 1985

Dr. Albert Sabin, EEUU, inventor de la vacuna oral contra la polio —1985

Dr. Albert Sabin, Etats-Unis Responsable de la mise au point du vaccin oral anti-polio—1985

173

International Committee of the Red Cross—1986

Comité Internacional de la Cruz Roja —1986

La Commission Internationale de la Croix Rouge—1986

The Countess of Ranfurly, England Literacy Pioneer—1987

Condesa de Ranfurly, Inglaterra, pionera de la alfabetización —1987

La Comtesse de Ranfurly, Angleterre
Pionnier du mouvement d'alphabétisation—1987

The Salvation Army—1988

Ejército de Salvación —1988

L'Armée du Salut—1988

1989—No award
1989—Aucun récipiendaire choisi
1989—No se otorgó premio

*Vaclav Havel, Czechoslovakia
President, Czech and Slovak
Federative Republic—1990*

*Vaclav Havel, Checoslovaquia,
presidente de la República
Federativa Checa y Eslovaca —1990*

*Václav Havel
Président de la République fédéra-
tive tchèque et slovaque—1990*

*Javier Pérez de Cuéllar, Peru
United Nations Secretary General—
1991*

*Javier Pérez de Cuéllar, Perú,
secretario general de las Naciones
Unidas —1991*

*Javier Pérez de Cuéllar, Pérou
Secrétaire général des Nations
Unies—1991*

175

Glossary of Programs
Programs of Rotary International

Friendship Exchange: Through Friendship Exchange, Rotarians and their families enjoy reciprocal visits internationally. There are both club-to-club programs for individuals and district-to-district programs for larger groups. The purpose of Rotary Friendship Exchange is to advance international understanding, goodwill, and peace through people-to-people contacts across national boundaries.

Interact Clubs: Interact is a service club for young people of secondary-school age sponsored by a Rotary club. In addition to social activities, each Interact club carries out at least one local and one international service project each year.

International Vocational Contact Groups: Rotarians within the same business, profession, or vocational field associate with each other to further international fellowship and service. This pilot program expands the opportunities for Rotarians to serve through their occupations at an international level.

Preserve Planet Earth: The Preserve Planet Earth pilot program focuses the attention of Rotary clubs around the world on critical ecological issues. Clubs learn about threats to the environment and spread the word in their own communities. Diverse projects have been implemented around the globe to protect and restore ecological resources.

Rotaract Clubs: Rotaract is a service club for young adults between the ages of 18 and 29, sponsored by a Rotary club. Like Interact, Rotaract carries out at least one local and one international service project each year.

Rotary Village Corps: This innovative program encourages Rotary and Rotaract clubs to identify service-minded non-Rotarians with leadership potential who require organizational and technical assistance to carry out local development projects which improve the quality of community life.

Rotary Volunteers in Action (RVIA): RVIA matches individual Rotarian volunteers with situations in which their specific skills can be put to use. RVIA is centered within the community at the club level, but it also identifies volunteer opportunities at the district level and throughout the world.

Rotary Youth Leadership Awards (RYLA): RYLA is a program of seminars, conferences and camps to develop and recognize good citizenship and leadership qualities in young people. Selected participants between the ages of 14 and 30 meet with Rotarians and other resource people to exchange ideas, explore new career paths, learn how to arrange youth activities and community service projects, and discuss topics of importance to youth.

Youth Exchange: Rotary clubs and districts annually sponsor more than 9,000 young people of secondary-school age for travel and homestay with a Rotarian host family either for an academic year, during which the young person lives with more than one host family, or during an extended holiday of up to several weeks.

World Community Service (WCS): WCS links Rotary clubs needing help to complete a community service project with clubs in other countries willing to provide materials and technical and professional support. The Donations-in-Kind Information Network, a centralized system for publicizing the availability of donated goods and services to the Rotary world, was developed to enhance the WCS program.

World Fellowship Activities: Rotarians can expand their fellowship with Rotarians in other lands through membership in any of more than 25 World Fellowship Activities. These groups offer the opportunity to share interests in areas such as golfing, flying, computing, music, yachting, stamp collecting, and shortwave radio.

Programs of The Rotary Foundation of Rotary International

The objective of The Rotary Foundation of Rotary International is the achievement of world understanding and peace through international charitable and educational programs.

Ambassadorial Scholarships: The Rotary Foundation's Ambassadorial Scholarships provide support for students to spend an academic year abroad, continuing their studies, learning about other cultures, and serving as ambassadors of goodwill for Rotary and their countries. The program awards graduate, undergraduate and vocational scholarships, in a variety of fields of study. This is the oldest Foundation program, started in 1947.

Group Study Exchange (GSE): Paired teams of four or five young business and professional men and women—non-Rotarians—visit each other's country for four to six weeks to study economic, business, social and cultural conditions, generally staying in the homes of Rotarians. Team members share personal knowledge of their own country and of their professions and exchange ideas with those they meet. About 400 teams a year participate in this program begun in 1965.

Health, Hunger, and Humanity (3-H) Grants: The 3-H program marshals Rotary resources and manpower to accomplish large-scale, international projects that emphasize self-help and improve health, alleviate hunger, and enhance human and social develop-

ment. 3-H grants generally range from US$100,000 to $300,000 and last from one to five years.

Rotary Volunteers: This program, started in 1980, subsidizes the expenses of Rotarians, Foundation Alumni, and Rotaractors who volunteer their services and expertise in another country. They may be assigned to specific projects, identify their own service opportunities, or be requested for service by another Rotary club or district, or by a government or nonprofit organization.

Carl P. Miller Discovery Grants: These grants, administered through the Rotary Volunteers program, provide "seed money" in the form of travel and related expenses for the development of international Rotary service projects. Named for the past R.I president whose gift created the program in

1989, these grants support the direct people-to-people contact needed in a project's planning stages rather than funding the project itself.

Matching Grants: Matching funds are offered for small international, humanitarian, and charitable service projects conducted by Rotary clubs and districts. A project must involve active participation and partial funding (at least 50 percent) by clubs or districts in at least two countries, including a cooperating club or district in the benefiting country. The program was begun in 1965.

PolioPlus: The PolioPlus Program's goal is to help rid the world of poliomyelitis and to support efforts to control five other vaccine-preventable diseases. It provides polio vaccines and supports the social mobilization activities of Rotarians in about 100 developing nations. Po-

lioPlus gave impetus to the World Health Organization's target of global polio eradication, and Rotary hopes to celebrate its centennial year, 2005, in a polio-free world.

Rotary Grants for University Teachers to Serve in Developing Countries: Begun in 1985-86, grants of US$10,000 each have been provided each year to higher education faculty members to teach for six to ten months in a developing country.

Rotary Peace Programs: This program, started in 1987-88, offers a network of activities including international seminars and conferences that focus on the causes of conflict and activities that can enhance and improve the search for peace. The program seeks also to stimulate activities at the club and district level to promote peace and world understanding.

Glosario sobre programas
Programas de Rotary International

Intercambio Rotario de Amistad: gracias al Intercambio de Amistad, los rotarios y sus familias tienen la oportunidad de viajar a otros países y hospedarse en hogares rotarios. Existen dos tipos de intercambio: individual (entre clubes) y para grupos (entre distritos). La finalidad del Intercambio Rotario de Amistad radica en el fomento de la comprensión internacional, la buena voluntad y la causa de la paz, mediante el contacto directo entre los pueblos más allá de las fronteras nacionales.

Clubes Interact: Interact es una organización de clubes de servicio patrocinada por Rotary para jóvenes en edad de cursar estudios medios. Además de actividades sociales, cada Club Interact lleva a cabo anualmente al menos un proyecto de servicio a nivel local y otro a nivel internacional.

Agrupaciones Profesionales para Contactos Internacionales: rotarios que pertenecen a un mismo campo empresarial o profesional se relacionan entre sí a fin de fomentar el compañerismo internacional y el servicio. Este programa piloto amplía las oportunidades para que los rotarios presten servicio a ni-

vel internacional a través de sus ocupaciones.

Preservemos el Planeta Tierra: el programa piloto Preservemos el Planeta Tierra concita la atención de los Clubes Rotarios del mundo entero sobre problemas ecológicos de importancia crucial. Los clubes se informan debidamente sobre las amenazas que penden sobre el medio ambiente, alertando posteriormente a sus respectivas comunidades. En diversos sitios del mundo han sido implementados proyectos destinados a proteger y restaurar los recursos naturales del planeta.

Clubes Rotaract: Rotaract es una organización de clubes de servicio para jóvenes adultos con edades comprendidas entre 18 y 29 años. Cada uno de tales clubes es auspiciado por un Club Rotario. Al igual que los Clubes Interact, cada Club Rotaract debe desarrollar anualmente, al menos un proyecto de alcance local y otro internacional.

Grupos de Rotary para Fomento Vecinal: Este renovador programa anima a los Clubes Rotarios y Rotaract a identificar a personas no pertenecientes a Rotary con potencial

de liderazgo y dispuestas al servicio, proporcionándoles ayuda técnica y organizativa para llevar a la práctica proyectos de desarrollo destinados al mejoramiento de las condiciones de vida en la comunidad.

Voluntarios de Rotary en Acción (VREA): VREA pone en contacto a voluntarios rotarios con los proyectos que necesiten de sus servicios. VREA tiene su base a nivel de la comunidad, a nivel de club, aunque también identifica las oportunidades de prestar servicio voluntario a nivel distrital y mundial.

Seminarios de Rotary para Líderes Jóvenes (RYLA): RYLA es un programa de seminarios, conferencias y campamentos destinados al desarrollo y reconocimiento del civismo y las cualidades de liderazgo en la gente joven. Los participantes seleccionados, con edades comprendidas entre los 14 y 30 años, se entrevistan con rotarios y otras personas, a fin de intercambiar ideas, estudiar nuevos planes de orientación sobre carreras, aprender a organizar actividades para la juventud y proyectos de servicio en la comunidad, y discutir sobre temas de importancia para la gente joven.

Intercambio de Jóvenes: los Clubes Rotarios y distritos patrocinan

178

anualmente a más de 9.000 estudiantes de enseñanza media para cursar estudios en el extranjero alojándose con familias rotarias durante un año lectivo (durante el cual cada estudiante recibe hospedaje en casa de varias familias rotarias), o durante un período de vacaciones de varias semanas.

Servicio en la Comunidad Mundial (SCM): SCM pone en contacto a Clubes Rotarios que necesiten ayuda para completar un proyecto de servicio en su comunidad con clubes en otros países dispuestos a proporcionarles la asistencia material, técnica y profesional necesaria para dicho empeño. La Red de Información sobre Donaciones en Especie (RIDE), sistema centralizado de datos destinado a difundir ofrecimientos de donación de bienes y servicios ante el mundo rotario, fue creada a los efectos de ampliar los alcances del programa de SCM.

Actividades Mundiales de Com-pañerismo en Rotary: Los rotarios pueden hacer amistad con sus compañeros de otras tierras, mediante su participación en cualquiera de las más de 25 asociaciones de Actividades Mundiales de Compañerismo en Rotary. Estas asociaciones ofrecen la oportunidad de compartir intereses en común en áreas tales como golf, aviación, informática, música, náutica, filatelia, y radio-afición.

Programas de La Fundación Rotaria de Rotary International

Introducción:

El objetivo de La Fundación Rotaria de Rotary International consiste en lograr la paz y la comprensión internacional a través de sus programas educativos y filantrópicos.

Becas de Buena Voluntad: las Becas de Buena Voluntad de La Fundación Rotaria ofrecen la oportunidad a sus beneficiarios de cursar estudios en el extranjero durante un año lectivo, ya sea continuando sus estudios, adquiriendo más conocimientos sobre otras culturas y sirviendo en calidad de embajadores de buena voluntad para Rotary International y sus países. El programa otorga becas para estudiantes universitarios, gradudados y de entrenamiento profesional, en gran diversidad de campos de estudio. Este programa, que data de 1947, es el más antiguo de la Fundación.

Intercambio de Grupos de Estudio (GSE): equipos hermanados de cuatro o cinco hombres o mujeres dedicados a los negocios o profesiones, no pertenecientes a Rotary, efectúan visitas a sus respectivos países durante períodos de cuatro a seis semanas, a fin de estudiar las condiciones económicas, empresariales y sociales de sus respectivas naciones, alojándose generalmente en hogares rotarios. Los integrantes de cada equipo comparten su conocimiento personal de sus propio país y de sus profesiones, intercambiando asimismo ideas con sus anfitriones. En este programa, iniciado en 1965, participan aproximadamente 400 equipos al año.

Subvenciones del programa de Salud, Nutrición y Desarrollo Humano (3-H): el programa 3-H administra los recursos y la labor rotaria a los efectos de desarrollar proyectos internacionales a gran escala que pongan énfasis en la autoayuda, contribuyendo a mejorar la salud, aliviar el hambre y acrecentar el desarrollo humano y social. La cuantía de las Subvenciones 3-H oscila entre los 100.000 y los 300.000 dólares, siendo su duración máxima cinco años.

Voluntarios de Rotary: este programa, iniciado en 1980, subsidia los gastos de rotarios, ex becarios y ex participantes en programas de la Fundación, y rotaractianos que voluntariamente aportan sus servicios, conocimientos y experiencia profesionales a proyectos desarrollados fuera de su país. Podrán ser asignados a determinados proyectos, buscar ellos mismos plaza para prestar servicio, o responder a la demanda presentada por un Club Rotario, distrito, o una organización gubernamental o no lucrativa.

Subsidios "Discovery" del Fondo Especial Carl P. Miller: estos subsidios, administrados a través del programa Voluntarios de Rotary, suministran "fondos activadores" para sufragar gastos de viaje y anexos para el desarrollo de proyectos de servicio internacional de Rotary. Su nombre constituye un homenaje al ex presidente de RI cuya donación creara el programa en 1989. Estos subsidios, más que dotar de fondos a un proyecto en sí, financian los contactos persona a persona necesarios para las etapas de planificación de un proyecto.

Subvenciones Compartidas: se ofrecen fondos equivalentes a los aportados por Clubes Rotarios y distritos, a los efectos de desarrollar proyectos de servicio internacional a pequeña escala, de índole humanitaria y caritativa. Para hacerse acreedor a estas subvenciones, los proyectos deberán contar con la participación activa y financiación parcial (50 por ciento como mínimo) aportada por los clubes o distritos de los dos países participantes. Este programa dio comienzo en 1965.

PolioPlus: el objetivo del programa PolioPlus consiste en erradicar la poliomielitis de la faz de la tiera, apoyando asimismo los esfuerzos para mantener bajo control a otras cinco enfermedades inmunoprevenibles. Proporciona vacunas antipolio y apoya las actividades de movilización social de los rotarios en aproximadamente 100 países en desarrollo. PolioPlus dio impulso al objetivo de la Organización Mundial de la Salud de erradicación global de la polio. Rotary tiene esperanza en poder celebrar su centenario, en el año 2005, en un mundo libre de la amenaza de la polio.

Becas de Rotary para Profesores Universitarios para Dictar Cátedra en Países en Desarrollo: a partir de 1985-86, han sido concedidas anualmente becas por una cuantía de 10.000 dólares cada una a docentes universitarios, para impartir enseñanza en un país en desarrollo durante períodos de seis a diez meses de duración.

Programas pro Paz de Rotary: Este programa, que data de 1987-88, ofrece una vasta red de actividades entre las cuales se incluyen seminarios internacionales y conferencias dedicadas a dilucidar las causas de los conflictos, y las posibles actividades destinadas a luchar más efectivamente por la causa de la paz. Este programa procura asimismo estimular actividades a nivel de club y de distrito a fin de promover la paz y la comprensión internacional.

Glossaire
PROGRAMMES DU ROTARY INTERNATIONAL

Echanges amicaux : Dans le cadre des Echanges amicaux, des Rotariens et leur famille effectuent des visites réciproques, résidant chez des familles rotariennes étrangères. Il s'agit respectivement d'un programme de club à club conçu pour des particuliers et d'un programme de district à district conçu pour des groupes. Le but des Echanges amicaux du Rotary est d'accroître l'entente internationale, la bonne volonté et les relations amicales parmi les peuples du monde.

Clubs Interact : Interact est un club de service réunissant des lycéens. Le programme est parrainé par un Rotary club local. En plus des activités sociales, chaque club Interact mène à bien au moins un projet de service local et international chaque année.

Groupes internationaux de contacts professionnels : Les Rotariens de même milieu d'affaires ou de même profession peuvent se rencontrer pour accroître les possibilités de camaraderie et de service internationaux. Ce programme pilote élargit les possibilités qu'ont les Rotariens de servir au niveau international grâce à leur profession.

Protégeons notre planète : Ce programme pilote s'intéresse aux problèmes critiques de l'écologie. Les clubs s'informent des dangers que court l'environnement et informent leur communauté. Divers projets environnementaux ont été mis en place dans le monde pour protéger et restaurer les ressources naturelles.

Clubs Rotaract : Rotaract, un club de service, rassemble de jeunes adultes âgés de 18 à 29 ans. Le programme est parrainé par un Rotary club. Comme Interact, Rotaract mène à bien au moins un projet de service local et international chaque année.

Les Unités de développement communautaire : Un programme innovateur dans le cadre duquel des Rotary clubs et clubs Rotaract parrainent par une aide technique des organisations d'hommes et de femmes désireux de servir et travaillant ensemble pour améliorer la qualité de la vie des communautés rurales et urbaines de leur région.

Les Volontaires du Rotary en action (VRA) : Ce programme pilote met en contact des bénévoles rotariens avec des projets où leurs qualifications sont nécessitées. Bien que ce programme se concentre principalement au niveau du club, il localise également des possibilités de volontariat au sein du district et dans le monde.

Initiatives rotariennes pour une promotion de la jeunesse : Le RYLA (sigle anglais) est un programme qui grâce à des séminaires, conférences et camps de formation de cadres, contribuent à développer — et à récompenser — les qualités civiques et le sens des responsabilités des jeunes. Les jeunes gens sélectionnés, âgés de 14 à 30 ans, rencontrent des Rotariens pour explorer ensemble des sujets d'importance pour la jeunesse, examiner de nouvelles filières professionnelles et apprendre à organiser des projets d'Action d'intérêt public.

Echange de jeunes : Chaque année, les Rotary clubs et districts parrainent plus de 9.000 lycéens, qui vont voyager à l'étranger et séjourner chez des Rotariens soit pendant une année d'étude, durant laquelle l'étudiant peut vivre dans plus d'une famille, soit pendant des vacances scolaires de quelques semaines.

Action d'intérêt public mondial : L'Action d'intérêt public mondial met en contact des Rotary clubs ayant besoin d'aide pour mettre en oeuvre un projet de service avec des clubs étrangers désireux de fournir du matériel et un support technique ou professionnel. Pour les aider, le Rotary a établi le **Réseau d'information des dons en nature**, qui publie la liste des biens, fournitures et services offerts par les Rotariens et Rotary clubs pour être utilisés par d'autres clubs et districts dans leurs projets de service.

Amicales rotariennes mondiales : Des possibilités de rencontre sont offertes aux Rotariens qui appartiennent aux quelque 25 Amicales rotariennes mondiales. Ces groupes leur offrent l'occasion de partager leur passion, telle que le golf, les sports aéronautiques, l'informatique, la philatélie ou la CB.

PROGRAMMES DE LA FONDATION ROTARY DU ROTARY INTERNATIONAL

L'objectif de la Fondation Rotary du Rotary International est d'accroître l'entente internationale et les relations amicales parmi les peuples du monde grâce à des programmes humanitaires et éducatifs.

Bourses d'études : Les boursiers vont tous étudier dans un pays étranger pendant une année universitaire. Ils sont des ambassadeurs de bonne volonté du Rotary. Ce programme accorde des bourses pour des études de licence, post-licence et professionnelles, ainsi que dans de nombreux autres domaines. C'est le plus ancien programme de la Fondation, débuté en 1947.

Echanges de groupes d'étude : Dans ce programme, des équipes de jeunes professionnels non-rotariens partent à l'étranger pendant quatre à six semaines pour étudier les conditions sociales, économiques, professionnelles et culturelles du pays d'accueil, tout en séjournant dans des foyers rotariens. Ils partagent leurs connaissances de leur pays et de leur profession. Environ 400 groupes par an participent à ce programme débuté en 1965.

Programme "La Santé, la faim et l'humanité" : Le programme 3-H (Health, Hunger and Humanity) mobilise les ressources et les bras du Rotary pour accomplir des projets de service internationaux à grande échelle basés sur l'auto-assistance et qui ont pour but d'améliorer la santé, de soulager la faim et de développer les conditions sociales de l'homme. Le montant des subventions 3-H s'élève de 100.000 à 300.000 dollars EU pour des projets s'étendant de un à cinq ans.

Les Volontaires du Rotary : Ce programme de la Fondation, débuté en 1980, offre à des Rotariens, des anciens bénéficiaires de la Fondation et des Rotaractiens l'occasion d'utiliser leur expérience pour un service humanitaire à l'étranger. Ils peuvent être envoyés vers un projet spécifique, trouver leur propre occasion de service, ou bien être appelés par un autre Rotary club ou district, un gouvernement ou une organisation philanthropique.

Les Subventions "Découverte" Carl P. Miller : Elles sont gérées dans le cadre du programme des Volontaires du Rotary. Nommées en l'honneur de l'ancien président du Rotary International dont la donation permit la création de ce programme en 1989, ces subventions permettent à des Rotary clubs ou districts d'effectuer un voyage d'études nécessaire avant de développer de nouveaux projets de service internationaux. Elles parrainent les contacts de personne à personne nécessaires avant de démarrer un projet.

Subventions de contrepartie : Ces subventions sont conçues pour des projets éducatifs ou humanitaires parrainés et partiellement financés (au moins à 50%) par des Rotary clubs ou district de deux ou plusieurs pays. Un des Rotary clubs ou districts se trouve dans le pays bénéficiaire. Le programme a débuté en 1965.

Programme PolioPlus : PolioPlus apporte son aide à des programmes étendus d'immunisation contre d'autres maladies évitables par vaccination dans les pays en voie de développement, en coopération avec l'Organisation mondiale de la santé, l'UNICEF et les autorités nationales et régionales de la santé. Ils participent également à des activités de "mobilisation sociale", qui incitent le public et le secteur privé ainsi que des milliers de volontaires à mener à bien des campagnes de vaccination. Le Rotary International espère célébrer son 100ème anniversaire, qui aura lieu en 2005, dans un monde libéré de la polio.

Subventions pour professeurs d'université : Depuis 1985, les districts rotariens peuvent aussi fournir une subvention de 10 000 dollars E.U. à un professeur d'université allant enseigner dans un pays en voie de développement entre six et dix mois.

Forums du Rotary pour la Paix : Ce programme pilote consiste en une série de rencontres pour examiner le rôle que le Rotary et d'autres organisations non-gouvernementales peuvent jouer pour atteindre la paix dans le monde et pour soutenir les efforts de groupes travaillant dans ce sens. Depuis 1988, ces forums cherchent à accroître la compréhension des conflits pour trouver des solutions, et à stimuler la promotion de la paix par le biais de projets.

Partners in Service
Colaboración para el servicio
Partenaires dans le service

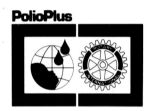

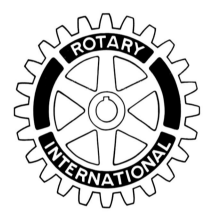